STEEL THE DARKNESS

by

Dana G Smith

Preface to Steel the Darkness

I would like to thank my wife and companion for her help in this book. I personally thank her for her efforts in editing, proof reading, making suggestions, and in joining me in this publication.

We hope you will enjoy this book for what it is. A journey, a story, and one filled with characters which fill the path you will take. It has been a true joy to write this book to create characters and to present to you, the reader a story set in modern America.

You will be taken on a journey filled with Dark powers, Lucifer, and those who follow him who are bent on taking over the America of which we write. The battle is set as Remnant Christians, a Jewish Prophet, historical powers from the beginning of this nation, along with UFO's, Nephilim, and other people make up the bulk of this story. The two sides are fighting a battle. Two forces, many principalities, prophecies, dark shadows, the power of God, and His Son Jesus Christ; Yeshua HaMassiach all move together in this epic story of survival, faith, and power!

Thanks to the Lord Jesus Christ for all he has done in my life and those of my family, and of the brethren whom I have known.

Mr. Dana G Smith
WIBR/WARN Media
www.DanaGlennSmith.com
www.Warn-Usa.com

Chapter One: The Light of Day

And in that day, they shall roar against them like the roaring of the sea: and if one look unto the land, behold darkness and sorrow, and the light is darkened in the heavens Isaiah 5:30

The sun beat down on the sandstone colored tiles that made the pathway up to the adobe brick home. It was hot and in the distance, you could see heat waves rising. It looked like Hades had come to the area. Indeed, this portion of Arizona had gotten hot hovering around the 115 to 120 marks. The messenger knocked on the door. He looked around and saw no one. There were no cars, no sign anyone was home. He was now standing on the veranda and a cool mist hit him and he looked up. Vines covered the ceiling and in their midst, he could see small lines that sprayed the mist out. A good way to cool down he thought.

"Urgent Message Colonel;" he waited a moment then heard a shuffling inside, "Okay, Okay"

He had driven two hours to get here and along the way he entered the villa ground which if you called it that, was strange. Several four wheelers sat parked under the shade tree to the right. The messenger looked around and surveyed the tall fence with barbed wire at the top which surrounded this villa. He thought to himself "why would you need this security, there is nothing here". As he pondered where he was he figured that at least 50 square miles of desert stretched out in all directions from this main house. Then there was the entry way with a guard shack that allowed no one to enter except for those on the list. He saw a few out buildings; nothing else. He had no idea why this was here and this made him wonder! Above him and to the left was a high definition security camera, it blended in and was placed just right as to bring little attention. He would not have noticed it, but in the absence of nothing else to do; he was looking everything over closely.

Within a moment the heavy door swung open and there stood the medium stature Colonel in a clean crisp uniform, which had no dirt or wrinkles. He was all business and his demeanor at once unsettled the messenger. No one really knew much about him, but one thing was sure, he did not like visitors.

"Yes, give it to me" gruffly the Colonel spoke as he gazed into the eyes of the messenger. "You're new to this, huh?"

"Yes sir, Colonel" said the messenger who shifted his weight from one foot to the other and nervously looked away.

"Here is a tip, now beat it" the Colonel said irritatingly and the young messenger looked at a fifty-dollar bill. With that, the messenger disappeared.

Opening the envelope, there was no return address, but it was government stock paper. Inside was the sentence "Get here quick, meeting urgent, details when you arrive".

The Colonel paused for a moment, thinking on the words. He liked his space and his privacy. No one would or could just sneak up in his world. He went into his study and laid down the message and then went into the security room across the hallway. The complex system of security with several men sitting before myriad of screens and communication equipment lay before the Colonel. On one monitor the Colonel saw that the young messenger was out on the road headed to the entry gate where he came in at. He spoke to one of the soldier's and said, "give me a close up of him Steve". The soldier looked at the Colonel and then quickly focused the cam for a closer look. "Snap a picture of him. Be sure to double check the plate number; be sure he is really from the agency who is supposed to be handling the communiques. Also run a full security check on him, call his boss. I want details and everything there is about him. I want to know what toothpaste he uses." "Will do Colonel", replied the soldier who then began a series of encrypted email communications. The lines were direct within the bases and secure.

The Colonel smiled to himself as he thought about the fact that this young man had no clue as to what was really going on here. The Colonel loved the secrecy, the projects, and the power. Ah, yes the power; that makes this worth it all. When he speaks, people listen. When he gives orders, they are carried out and if he want's someone dead; well that is in the normal routine of things here. He was dangerous and he knew it. But this messenger who now is far away in the distance had no idea of who he was just talking too and the Colonel wanted it that way. Down the hall and to the right, the Colonel opened a door and went down the stairs. At the end of the corridor was an elevator, he entered and it descended. The doors swung open and the Colonel was greeted by a soldier and a crisp salute. "Greetings Colonel are you headed out?" the soldier looked at the Colonel when he spoke and adjusted his stance.

"Yes Brad, are my things still packed" questioned the Colonel

"Yes sir" was the reply accompanied by another crisp salute

Brad was the Colonel's longtime assistant. He stood six feet five, pressed weights, and looked like a linebacker for some pro football team. He had a square jaw, blonde hair, and had a hand shake like a vise. He was well versed in martial arts, an expert marksman, and had a master's degree in philosophy.

"Good, let us get going" replied the Colonel

They both went side by side, quietly and moved into the rail area. As they came into the overlook and onto the main arena the silver bullet train came into view. The trains have been developed in the black ops budget and never have seen the light of day. They were designed and built, then modified all in the confines of the bunker. They are at level 12 and the train was built to ride by magnetism, being propelled and kept on the tracks all at the same time. The train maintains a separate pressurized atmosphere. Traveling in a vacuum rail tube, the system provides for friction free move-ability. The train literally lifts up and provides a smooth ride at an incredible speed. It is fast, very fast and although the technology was finally released, the main portion that makes this train superior was kept secret. But the nations of the world have jumped on this type of speed and even

China is now developing its own train. But what they don't know is what they have in this system. The specs say this train moves at speeds of 1500 mph and is all done underground. But the system can go two to three times faster than that. The whole system is built and maintained by the black project he heads. The Colonel entered the train and sat in the main area. A red phone with direct links to the President, Joint Chiefs, and the Pentagon all stood ready on the desk besides the chair he sat down in. A bar sat in the corner and two armed men stood at the corner of the room waiting for the train to move. A huge screen was in against the wall in front of him and beside it sat a computer terminal and all sorts of buttons, devices, and communication equipment. The Colonel was not the wiz at that stuff, he was the impetus. He simply got the job done. He had a reputation to protect. If the black ops needed someone to get it done, it was he. The Colonel smiled as he thought on these things. Surely, he mused to himself "how ignorant are the citizens of this land". Sitting back he reached for a new prepared Espresso of Belgian coffee and heavy cream, with a shot of schnapps. He felt himself moving as the bullet proof windows to the side were a blurred picture of the concealment structure the train used. He sat back, pushed a small button and the windows instantly covered over with a hard titanium covering. Now, safe in his cocoon, he would make it there in no time.

The window of the coffeehouse let in the Wyoming sun. The perfect summer weather in the high country felt good as Gin looked around to see if her contact had arrived. She had a picture of him and her people had decided to meet in a familiar popular coffee house here in Jackson. She looked at the pic once again to keep the figure in mind so she would recognize him, no mistakes here. Record snow this past winter in the high country had melted making everything green, colorful, and lush in Jackson Hole. The harsh snowy winter had made for great skiing and the town had been very busy with tourists. But now in July the summer had arrived full blown. It was not so hot, but it was beautiful. The Snake River which ran full, as did other streams, due to the heavy snowmelt had now returned to their normal flow. Now it was River Rafting, hiking, biking, fishing, and all the summer sports that made things around this neck of the woods so popular. This was especially true of Jackson Lake, whose waters were cold, crystal clear and full of trout. This made for popular attraction in the summer months.

Gin loved to ski, and had taken advantage of the powder this last winter when she had time to come up here. But now, she dressed the part of summer with a cool top and shorts, wearing some sandals with nice bead work on them. She had picked up the outfit and shoes in Jackson from one of the many shops. Gin loved it here; the closeness to nature, and the shopping. Jackson had a big town feel to it, but also a smaller town atmosphere. But this was not one of those getaway trips she likes to have. You know, the one's where you could go and have fun and relax. She was here on business and the Reverend had given her the scoop. Gin worked as a liaison for the group headed by the Rev as people called him. They had an opportunity to get some important info on the Colonel. But she had dressed somewhat provocatively as to use every bit of advantage she could. At a time when society pushed women to be manlier, Gin was one that enjoyed the sex God gave her. She was all woman and liked it that way! It is her feminine charms that she would use, but in a very lady like way. Gin would be lovely and innocent, but sharp, full of wit and smart, getting the information, the Rev needed. All without so much as a wonder from anyone as to her real motives here. "But if you're doing important work", she thought; "you might as well have a great tasting French pastry in the process". This was why she now sat at a table near a window in full sun. She was watching everyone as they passed by to find her contact with whom she would meet. The small shop was very popular, especially in the morning and afternoons. They simply had the best coffee and French pastries she ever tasted. As she watched from her table, Gin saw a slim figure of a man on the sidewalk in front of the window where she sat. She tapped on the window and the man turned around, Gin held up the picture and it was her contact. He noticed her and held up his pic of her. In a short while, he came to the table where she sat. The both sat for a long moment looking at each other. A waitress interrupted the silence and dropped off a couple of waters and a menu. Gin acknowledge her and took up the menu, her contact following her lead began to peruse the coffee's flavors on the board at the front. There were lined up customers who were busy at a large and very long glass case filled with all the best French pastries there were. The owners had come over directly from France and on a trip to Jackson Hole, fell in love with the place. They made all the arrangements to come to America and today, some twenty years later; the place was the staple of fine French pastries in the whole of the Rocky Mountains.

From across the street, conspicuously hid; a tall cowboy figure stood in the shade of the tree. The brim of his hat was pulled down just enough to see and in the process, hide his face. He had seen the young slender woman go into the shop. She was dressed in some shorts and a top that highlighted her figure very well. He was impressed, and man she had nice looking legs. He also saw her pull up at one of the windows that looked out onto the sidewalk and sit at a table. Despite her apparent charm and good looks, he was not here for that. He thought he had recognized her, but he was here to make sure the contact was made. He was a handler, the go between the General and the man they used to infiltrate certain people of interests. This job was to get information on a group headed up by a man nicknamed "the Rev". His man was about to make contact and now he saw his man just sitting down at a table in the sun. He turned just enough to make a call without being noticed. The phone rang and a voice answered, "Yes"

"Contact made sir"

"Good, stay on them, but out of sight; don't do a thing; but make sure your man doesn't blow it. Report any new developments ASAP."

Meanwhile, in the coffee shop; the pair seemed not to have noticed they were being watched. After some small talk, Gin and her contact sat sipping their hot drinks. Each had picked a fresh made delicacy from among the different croissants, napoleon's, donuts, and fresh fruit cream tarts arranged neatly on the tray that the server had brought around. They both had chosen a bold and dark French roast from among the various coffees offered. Gin put a shot of heavy cream in hers, but her companion drank his black.

"I was given a picture of you, but nothing prepared me to see you in shorts." he said looking at Gin; then he asked, "You come to Jackson often?"

"Well, yes I do come here off and on, I love the ambience of Jackson surrounded by the mountains; plus, Grand Teton. I must also say your picture does not do you justice. You are better looking in person." Gin smiled, revealing her white teeth and small lips. She could tell he was looking her over, 'Good' she thought, it is always better to disarm your opponent".

"I am glad you decided to meet here, love the pastries and coffee. I am a gourmet, of sorts; with coffee. I buy the best beans, roast them myself. I know great coffee and this is great stuff, but mind you; it is not as good as mine" He laughed as he spoke smiling back at Gin. He really liked this meeting; he had dreaded who he would meet here. Glad it was her, he thought.

Gin noticed his dark thick black hair shining in the sun, his lips were moistened by the coffee and she looked him over. Indeed, he was very good looking, probably 'about my age and not too bad', she thought.

"Indeed, this is the best coffee and fresh pastries around" Gin retorted, and then in a more serious tone looked at her contact and said, "What information do you have for the Rev?"

"I have some information on a remote location Ranch in Wyoming. It is used by the Colonel and his people. The problem is traceability, it is impossible to pinpoint the Colonels group as the owners. But we know they carry out assignments, hits, and other stratagems for their projects from here. It is just one of many such places they use and very hush, hush. I had trouble even getting people to talk about it, until one day I ran into some guys off base. It was then I was led to the file and more info which I have for you". He handed Gin the file

with the information he had with him. Gin saw an official

Government seal and the words "Top Secret" and it prompted her to

grab the file and quickly put it down inside her bag she had with her.

Her contact saw her react and then continued to describe what he

knew of the file, but in a lower more cautious manner; "The whole

Ranch and its holdings revolve around a secret deed, I mean if you

looked for it by standard methods and titles; it would never come up.

It would be listed as a proprietary land used for research by; and get

this; the University of Wyoming. Can you believe that, I mean tying

the Colonels land to the only major university in Wyoming is crazy?

But that is what they have done, somehow! But if you go do the

research, it is not there either; I mean no other information. Nothing,

zilch, nada! For all intents and purposes, the facility is totally secret,

totally off limits to anyone wanting to enter it."

"That is all we need in this state, a place for the Project and their

cold-blooded killers to hang out. Especially the Colonel, I mean he

would slice up his own grandmother if he thought it would help his

projects any", Gin stopped speaking and finished off the rest of her croissant." She noticed a suspicious figure as she looked out the window. There was a shadow in a shadow.

"Somebody is over there, see him? Is he watching us?" Gin questioned her contact

"I don't know, hard to tell, but wouldn't put it past them"

"You weren't followed, were you? You know they will kill anyone suspected of interfering. We have already lost some great people." Gin worried now as she strained to see the figure, but it was gone! She then looked directly at her contact and asked, "by the Way how do you know the Reverend in order to contact him?"

"Well, let's just say we have a common enemy and a bond. We go way back, and that is all I can say!" He stopped and was now nervous.

Gin saw him beginning to look troubled, and then asked him "Where is the land?"

"The land itself is 5000 acres, both private and a parcel of it, is deeded on National Forest land. Also coming into play is an old Wyoming Ghost town, which is used as a cover. But to get to it, it takes a bit of doing! Now remember these things are not written in stone, this is our best information here. The real facility could be located anywhere. Yet our source inside says it is in Wyoming, close to the Montana border as well." He nervously looked around as he spoke. The place was busy and no one seemed to be interested in what they were doing. 'Good', he thought, and then handed a large envelope to her, saying "here is all the information and details, you guys can look it all over and get back to me if you need anything else, the Rev knows how to get in touch with me!"

As Gin and her contact spoke, they were again being watched; but from a different location. As the handler watched the two, he could tell his man was just too comfortable with this gal. She had gained the advantage simply by her looks. The Cowboy watched and was irritated, he softly spoke to himself. 'Shut up man, stop talking, you're giving this girl the in-depth story of your life. Man, he thought; this is irritating. This kid is just an amateur. I don't like to depend on such inexperience, but the General had put this kid in place and now he was doing big time stuff and if there were any mistakes, well he would just deep six him in the Snake over yonder.' He smiled to himself as he thought on these things, and continued to watch casually the meeting taking place not far from where he stood amongst the shadows.

"Well I have got to go!"

Gin looked at her contact who by now was looking out the window himself and he seemed to see something. "Yes, so do I", she replied as her contact finished quickly and got up. He nervously put a tip on the table and Gin saw him looking out the window and then she saw a large cowboy figure in the distance, and yes, he seemed to be watching. Her contact had indeed gotten upset and was visibly nervous.

"So long, enjoyed the time, but got to go", with that he went out the door. Gin watched him, until he disappeared out of sight. She sighed a bit, 'glad it was over' she thought to herself.

Gin's contact had made his way around the corner and was thinking about the girl he just met. He liked her and wondered if they would meet again. Yet, he had to be careful and now as he walked he looked for anyone suspicious. Then as he crossed an ally way, he came face to face with the reason why he was here in the first place.

"Get in here quick" the voice said

There in front of him was his handler who was dressed in a cowboy hat, chaps, and boots, looking like something out of the old west. He was the one in the shadows who had been watching.

"Did you give her all of it?"

"Yes just like you instructed me, but are you sure these people are as dangerous as you say? I mean she is nice, real nice!" he stopped and looked up, a stern face with no emotion stared at him through clinched teeth. A tall figure loomed over him, his presence was sinister and his demeanor even worse, this made the young man visibly nervous. But in a clench, he was a fighter, very tough, and even this guy could be brought down. But for now, he played things safe. He had gotten out of the service after his finished his tour in Afghanistan. After some months of lying around, out of the blue a government official contacted him. He had a chance to sign up for some black operations in America. It was all hush, hush; and above Top Secret but they told him "your just the kind we want, your service record shows your skills and duty to America." He had signed up, but it had from the start been very troubling in what he saw had been going on. There was something different about this government black operations project and the military he was in. The enemy now was Americans, including Christians, Pastors, patriots, constitutionalists, and anyone else they deemed a danger to the American way of life. As he stood there, his handler did not smile.

He never smiled. He now began to smile just at the thought of this guy always mad, always angry, and always seemed to be yelling for some reason. He yelled more than his sergeant at boot camp.

"Yea, what you are smiling about?" The handler smugly asked

"Oh, nothing, just enjoying the beautiful scenery here in downtown Jackson!" he replied

"You talk too much Kid! I saw you yammering at her. You were fawning over her weren't you! You amateurs are all alike, emotions. You let them in. This is business, plain and simple. Don't forget who you are talking too, I am your handler. If things don't go well, it is my job and responsibility here. Yes, maybe she is good looking and nice to you, but do not let such things deter you. Don't forget why we sent you down here. You are to get in with the leaders, gain their confidence, and find out their plans. We want names, numbers, descriptions, and the whole ball of wax. You did well in Afghanistan under cover, why would you have trouble in this little po-dunk state?"

He looked puzzled at his handler, then said; "I know very well what I was doing and yes she was good looking and if I enjoy myself by having a great cup of coffee, fine French pastry, and all with a pretty girl; what is it to you if I do my job? Besides, I was in deep cover in those days in Afghanistan and I know very well how to handle myself and don't call me kid! On top of all that these people can do nothing to stop you. You have forces and powers no man or nation can withstand, why these guys". He stopped and knew he had said too much, his anger had taken over and now his handler quieted down.

"I know your experience; just do as you're told! I follow orders and you are to do the same. I guarantee you that if you don't I will be forced to take care of It." The handler stopped and caught his breath. His anger subsided and his red face was regaining a normal color. But the handler added with a firm poke into the chest of his man; "Do you catch my drift here, and this is project law; sonny! The bottom line here is do as your told or there won't be enough left of you to feed the crows. You are not to be making observations, you are to do your job; no questions asked. Remember this is for the greater good"!

The young man looked up at the towering figure, the one he knew only as his handler and spoke "yes, of course, for the greater good. I understand quite well and will finish the mission"! He stopped and in his pocket his fingers had been crossed, a little white lie; and even now the heat was more than he bargained for. What was all this about? He looked up and saw the man pull away satisfied with his answer, and then quickly disappeared into the crowd of people on the busy sidewalk. He watched his head until he could see no more. He thought about following him, but decided against it. His handler would be in touch and would want some pertinent information or else. He had time and knew if he had to, he also could get lost. But he did not know just how dangerous the group was that he had joined. Whatever it was, it was not your normal government stuff, nor was it standard army! He knew enough to know, it was now too dangerous not to follow orders. He had to think of this and how to get out of what he had now joined. It was not for America, nor for the good of Americans. Whatever it was, it was a secret!

The train pulled to a stop. As it did the Colonel put the finishing touches on a second drink and sipped it slowly. He looked out as his aid pushed the button to raise the window covers and as the train slowed down you could see the walls of the enclosure. The doors opened and they walked out onto the terrace and there in the distance were some well-lit offices with people milling about. Security was everywhere and the place was abuzz. This was like grand central station, yet many floors beneath the earth; the Colonel thought. He made his way to the main office and found a seat in the chair opposite the man, as many called him. Two stars lay on his shoulders and the older Major General Tommy Johnson eyed the Colonel closely. The chain of command is swift and tough here. He is a no-nonsense commander and he answers directly to Gen. Edward Meyers who is in charge of NAMO, North American Operations.

"We have contacted them" General Johnson said strongly, rolling around a Cuban cigar in his mouth.

"You have, how?" questioned the Colonel

"We used a plant, furnished him with false information, but enough of it was real that they would not know the difference. He has made contact and they seemed to have taken the bait." The General sat back and rolled his chair.

The Colonel smiled an evil grin and said; "Really, that's great", then looking directly at the General he asked, "what do you want me to do?"

He looked over the Colonel, noticing that his cold and calculated manner took over as the General said distinctly; "We are well in handling the situation, but if anything should go south, so to speak;

we will need some cleanup"

"Yes sir, my specialty, I will take care of it" said the Colonel quickly

"You are responsible, no screw ups, cleanly done, no ties" the

General reminded him

"Yes, I know, why the worry", the Colonel looked around the room

as he heard footsteps in the hallway. He then looked back to the

General, who was just blowing out some smoke. The General had a

satisfied look on his face.

"These are the best Cubans I have had, they have outdone

themselves" General Johnson finished and took another puff and

looked again at the Colonel then answering him, said; "Because

these guys are getting to close to the truth, we must delay them until

Project Black Light is finished, and then they will have nothing to

say or do."

"Okay, sounds like a plan General", the Colonel stopped short as the

General asked him "How are the other programs doing there in the

desert?"

"Well, everything is going along smoothly; weapons, infiltration,

cloning, assassinations, and cover-ups. So far, we have placed our people in many of the designated areas that we targeted. Soon our people will be those "principalities in high places" the bible warned about, chuckling; the Colonel saw the General was not amused. The General was not a new comer to Christianity and the theology behind it. In fact, one-time years ago; he had graduated from a Presbyterian Seminary.

"Don't mock these...these...

"Christians" the Colonel snarled, the mere thought made a change in him, a dark and furious change. He wanted to kill, and the thought of the Christians and their God did this to him. But the Colonel quickly composed himself. He could control it, think clearly, and then rid himself of any enemy around that threatened him. These Christians are the enemy and the Colonel knew how to get rid of them.

The General grasp his cigar in his teeth, looking at the hatred in the Colonels eyes. He knew that hatred, it was well entrenched in many on the project. But they must not let emotions ruin the end goal. He looked sternly at the Colonel and spoke loudly to emphasize to the Colonel his point; "No they are not Christians like you may know. These people are called the Remnant, they are not taken in by the many things most churches and American Christians are. They know what darkness is, they know what we are planning. They have power. And something else; the Prophet".

The loud words came directly to the Colonel and had the intended effect. The Colonel shook himself and looked up, saying; "Really General, I did not think you worried like that. Give me a location and I will take my best men. In short order we will remove your problems."

"Colonel Listen; it is not that easy, these people take the bible literally and unlike many other Churches and groups, they have found secrets in their Word of God. They move around, are secretive and have some of the top scientists and researchers on their team. Besides you and I both know we cannot go around and just kill everyone we don't like, this is; after all, still America!" The General finished, then added; "And for some reason even our dark priests and prophets have no control over them. They seem helpless." The Generals voice quieted down as he waited for the Colonel to say something.

After a moment, the Colonel spoke in a gruff voice. "For a short time, this is still America, but there will come a day and we both know it, it will be finished. Plus, there is one power that can stop them, we have their own Word of God as proof, saying He will make war with them and overcome them; you and I both know who He is". Abruptly the conversation ended, and then the General motioned him on and said, "Yes we do, now get going Colonel, we will let you know soon of the progress." In the hallway, the Aide of the General had heard some of what was going on and soon saw the Colonel. Leading the way, the Aide made sure there was a clear path for him. He knew the Colonel was ready to get out of the place. But soon the Colonel was sipping another drink, settling down to relax as the train headed back to his home base Alpha.

Tiger came into the parking lot and got out. It had been a very long drive to the far outpost to which he had just come from. Who is this guy? He is one of the company's best customers; he pays double to make sure all deliveries are private and personal. He tips well, but why out there? These are questions that have been on Tigers mind ever since he found that place not too long ago, which is why he got this job in the first place. When he had seen the place, there was something odd about it that sparked his curiosity. This was not new for Tiger; he was a proverbial snooper and hacker. As a result, Tiger had purposed to find out why it was so restricted. They must be hiding something and as he thought a moment; a voice abruptly stopped his chain of thought. Looking up, he saw his boss.

"Tiger, Tiger, wake up and stop daydreaming. Did you find him? I mean how could you miss it, your journey is plotted on the GPS."

Tiger realized he indeed had been lost in thought and saw his boss Andrew Schultz looking at him, "Yes I found him, got a fifty for a tip. Man, it is a long way; do you know who he is?"

"No, all details are classified, but I can tell you; he is with the government and as a private carrier for the government, we handle all things on a QT."

"The government, huh; man, that is interesting; what is going on out there, area 51 or something? I mean a gate with armed guards, a perimeter fence with barb all around it, a few outbuildings, and just main adobe structure. Plus, the fact you have at least fifty some acres surrounding the whole place and it is a restricted base of some sort, it has got me wondering."

Tiger's boss looked at him, then motioned with his finger to his lips, "keep this under your hat, but rumor has it, and I mean rumor; that it is a lead in to a large government underground base. People even say they see UFO's and other things flying in and out of the place. They fly in and out, but there is no runway, how is that possible." He smiled finishing up with this warning "Tiger do not go snooping around there, do not let your curiosity get the best of you." Andrew had known Tiger for many years, having known his mom. He hired Tiger because he needed a job and he like the young man. Tiger was curious, but he was honest and a hard worker. He had seen him get into trouble, being mischievous because of something he wanted to find out about. Tiger would make a great investigative reporter. "Tiger you did a good job today, take the rest of the day off and have a good weekend".

Tiger drove out onto the six-lane highway that he had come in on in a hurry to get home. He had some hacking to do and knew where to start. The very address that he had just came from. It was not by chance that he was very adept at getting into systems. Under all Tiger's many talents lay hidden one of the best computer hackers there was. He could hack anything digital! That was who he was and what he liked doing. He had done it many times and now His curiosity getting the best of him, Tiger would spend this weekend finding out why this place was so secretive. What did they hide? Why did they need to keep it quiet? Sure it was associated with the government, but something was not right and he still was curious? He had to find out, besides he had the private number and secret site access of the base that his boss uses to contact them in regard to shipments. He would trace the number and find an IP related to it. He could find anything. If it was a computer linked to any system, he could find it, hack it, and find what he needed. It was a natural ability; besides he had been doing this since a young kid. What Tiger did not know, however; was that the Colonel was way ahead of him and by now had a file of Tiger sitting on his desk before him. The Colonel took no chances and one policy he had, no one comes and goes on the base without him reading all there is to know about them. This was the Colonels security, it was Black Op's security, and for breaches of security; well there was the Colonel himself.

Gin drove past the Elk Refuge as she made her way out of Jackson. She looked down at her bad and the Top-Secret file lay out in the open, she pushed it deep inside the pocket to hide it. The mere presence of the file and the words Top Secret bothered her greatly. As she made her way the Grand Teton and its sisters in the range were formidable and stood as guards to the whole of Jackson Hole. She looked at the Tetons briefly, then looked back on the highway in front of her as she thought to herself. Only in this area could you find former Vice Presidents like Dick Cheney, movie stars like Harrison Ford, and so many millionaires, you would get tired of keeping track of them all. But also, you would find the original population, living in smaller homes in the city. Many who originally lived here did not like the growth of both people and money coming to the area. Already the land is taken up by either the government or the rich. There is lots of money here. They live on gated ranches, and live as anonymously as they can. If one were not to look close, a movie star, a former President, or some other celebrity could walk right past you and you would never know it. They dress the way they do on purpose, to be inconspicuous. But the truth is, Gin thought; the real Jackson, the one I knew as a kid; is gone, just like the America I used to know.

Years ago, her Pastor, who passed away recently, used to discuss, preach, and tell the congregation what was coming to the country. So many things have come true just like he said, like the one world government which you could tell was running America through the current Presidency now in place in the Oval Office. You could tell they feared the conservatives, gun right advocates, and Christians.

Just like in the old Roman Empire when the Caesars would blame Christians for anything bad that happened. It was in the Roman Empire where ten major persecutions of Christians went on and multitudes were killed in the most horrendous ways. Gin shuddered at the thought and made her way up on the rim and out of town. She was well out of Jackson and going towards Grand Teton Park. Suddenly her phone rang and she picked it up.

"Hi Mom, oh yes I am out of Jackson."

"Yep, I made my appointment and all is fine, I will be home in a few hours.

"Yes, Mom, I know you don't like me driving alone, but I am grown up now. I know you pray for me and I pray for you now don't worry, I will be home soon." Gin paused as she listened to her mother, then she said "Mom, I am driving; you know I don't like to talk on my cell and drive. I will talk with you when I get home. Yes, I know you love me, I love you too; good bye." Gin hung up and turned to see a car speed by her. As it passed the driver looked at her but as he saw her looking at him; he turned away quickly and sped on. Gin took a second look and the figure had a cowboy hat on and the vehicle was a truck. Like for Ranch work. The tags gave the description as from Sheridan County. Gin looked down and she was doing close to 70 and he passed her quickly. She did not like the look of the guy and thought to herself of the secret location that her contact had told her about. 'Could this guy be from there? Was he the one watching our meeting'? She thought again, and then shook it off, 'nah, just coincidence'. Mom was right it is not good for a young woman to be driving all alone. Yet she had faith and that faith was in the Lord, he would keep her safe. She believed that and had made the choice to be firm in that faith, believing that in all things her Lord would be with her.

Evenings in the Desert are great, it is quiet and the world of the night comes alive, thought the Colonel as looked out his window, and then strode to the door; opening it. He walked slowly to the four-wheeler parked over to the side of the house. He would take a ride. He started it up and soon he was riding to the gate, the guard nodded and saw that along with the Colonel were his aid and two other soldiers all on dirt bikes following him. The group went out the gate, off the pavement and onto the restricted land, which was well marked. As they drove, security camera's unseen by the human eye followed them from clumps of trees, shrubs, wildflowers, cactus, and other natural formations. The Colonel sped up and made his way through a maze of Barrel and Prickly pear cacti. The full moon cast a brilliant night light on the Arizona Sands which lit the place up. On nights like this you could see a long way. This was the best time for the Colonel, at night, on a full moon, in the desert southwest. He came upon a rise and looked out. From where he stood, he saw the Alpha B entrance opened and two lone figures were standing there. This was another secretive entrance that was made to look like the sand and fauna of the desert. With the mere human eye it was impossible to detect a doorway to the depths beneath the very sands the Colonel and his men were standing on. The Colonel told his men to stay and he went on by foot, walking slowly; looking at the ground for the not so friendly Black Rattlesnake or the sidewinder; not to mention all the other critters. The Colonel walked a few more yards and looked again; yes, as he thought; it was Elonah and Londo. As he looked at them, you could see their very tall figures clearly now. Their blonde hair also gleamed in the moonlight. Although it was quiet, the two stood there together not speaking. Yet their communication was not verbal this time. They were telepathic and communicated with each other, in an ongoing style which no one heard but the two communicating silently with each other.

"Do you see it Londo"

"Yes, I do"

"Pleiades, but look there is Orion"

"I know, it makes me want to go home", said Elonah softly

"There is nothing like the vast galaxies, stars, and constellations to make you want to do that"

"Go Home!"

"Yes, Home" agreed Londo "We will be finished one day with our work here"

"Then Home, I'm glad" said Elonah excited at the thought

"I will be glad as well!" replied Londo.

From high on a hill pushing out from the national forest, Mac could see the approaching night sky very clearly. He strained to see in the distance, 'good no approaching lights, no sign, nothing; which was just the way he liked it' he thought. It was dusk, turning to night. But even now some stars had made it out. All around it was still light enough to see the river glistening in the canyon below as it roared to its destination. Pine trees also stood out as sentinels, while the night pursued it course in nature to close down the day. Mac

turned and walked from his vantage point; seeing nothing that could

be construed as a danger. This was part of his makeup. He was

always on the lookout, he did not like surprises or unwanted

company. It was his background in the military and this had made

him more like a company commander than a friend when he went

camping or on an outing. He was always on the watch, on guard.

People noticed it, but his friends knew why he was the way he was,

they paid it no mind. Mac made his way into the camp and stood

over the fire that now had glowing white and red coals in it. The

camp coffee was done and the grounds he had tossed in it had settled

to the bottom of the pot. He liked a good hot cup or two in the

mountains at night while he enjoyed the stars, the mountains, and the

serenity. The coffee steamed and he blew on it as the cup warmed

his hands. Still in the high country, even in the summer; it does get

cold at night. Some places like Wind River Lake are still frozen in

early to late summer depending on the weather. 'Nothing surprises

me in this country', thought Mac. His canvas tent made a rippling

sound as a breeze came through the upper pines where his camp was

set up. Tomorrow he would break camp and make his way back to the Ranch. 'Man', he thought, 'this is great'! As he stood there a sound came from the tent.

"A mouse" the voice shouted

Mac knew that his companion Melissa who was an outdoors enthusiast would not quiet down until that dreaded mouse was corralled and out of the tent. "Just a minute Honey, I will be there and help you"

"Forget it; got him" a satisfaction in her voice, Melissa gently tossed the creature over against the nearest group of trees, "Now go find another home, this one is taken".

Early the next morning after a breakfast of wild berries and camp biscuits with honey, the pair headed out. As they slowly walked, leading their horses, they stopped and looked over the valley below. They had taken two of Mac's best horses for the trip. The river came down out of the mountains where they were at and looked like a sapphire ribbon curled around the meadow below and fed directly into the lake. The Sun was now about the eight o-clock position and the rocky ledge they were standing on gave way to a sheer drop. Moving away, Mac found the path which they had come up on the plateau where they stayed, it was a couple of feet wider than the horses. They headed towards the lake in the distance below. It would take four hours, even on horseback to get back home to the ranch, but they also would simply walk some; leading the horses as they took their time going downhill. They had spent a few days away from it all and now Melissa had to get back to work and Mac needed to check the ranch.

They had been some time on the trail and the two approached a meadow not far from the Ranch house. Mac now watched Melissa. Her blonde hair was braided and hung just beneath her shoulders. She was dressed in boots, tight jeans, and figure forming blouse covered in a Levi jacket. She wore a pink cowboy hat and looked at Mac watching her. She enjoyed it when he looked at her and she knew that Mac liked her; a lot. Mac smiled back and just looking at her made him appreciate the fact that they had a special bond between them. They spent a lot of time together and Mac was trying to tell Melissa of his past; but so far, he had been unable to find the words to tell her. But his affection for her was strong and although Mac would not admit to loving Melissa; he knew deep inside she was the woman for him. He loved her, although he could not admit it. They shared many private and personal moments together, just the two up in the woods alone. He liked it that way.

The ranch came into view. They had been on company property for quite a while now and the whole of the Ranch and adjacent land looked more like a hunting camp than anything else. It was as he wanted it. The log cabin house on the Ranch was made with pine logs. The house blended in with the forest that surrounded it. The natural stone pathway and stone fence also looked like they fit right in. A natural spring gurgled in the nearby pasture and a pipe went from the spring to the house. This was the summer range, in winter; everything was shut down and made ready for the severe cold and snow. He then would go to the winter shelter that ran rich with a hot mineral spring. This was located deep within mountains close to natural hot springs. It also was all private land and secluded.

Melissa after a kiss and a hug got in her SUV and cranked it up; she made her way out onto the main highway. The town was an hour away and soon she would be in a hot bath relaxing. She liked the time spent in the out of doors and she liked Mac, a lot. The time spent with him was special and Melissa had not been attracted to any man like she now was with Mac. They had kissed and shared many such moments. She especially liked them being alone together,

sitting close beside each other and looking out over the valleys

below. They would kiss, embrace, and feel that physical attraction; it

was special. It was in the mountains where love springs eternal and

Melissa knew she was well on her way with Mac. They had not had

sex, per se as many couples do today. They slept in the same tent,

but in separate sleeping bags. They never discussed marriage, but

Melissa thought about it but did not want to scare Mac off. But in

spite of all this, she really was falling in love with him; but she also

had something deep inside that told her Mac was hiding something

from her. Simply put, Melissa knew that she did not know all there

was to Mac. He was a nice guy, treated her great, and he seemed to

like her as well. But he was secretive, always looking out over a

ridge or from a cliff; like he was watching for something or

someone. Then Melissa remembered her encounter in town. She

had gotten done showing real estate to a group of interested buyers,

an investment they said; and then one of them spoke to her in

private. He pulled out a picture of Mac and she tried not to look

surprised or like she knew him. His name was Mike Anderson

President of Anderson Investments. Since she was in Real Estate, he figured she might have seen him. He was an old friend; he told her and wanted to find him again. He thought he bought a place near here, so he asked Melissa. Yet she did not trust him. Melissa hoped he did not notice the look on her face as she recognized the picture of Mac. Melissa did not tell him anything nor did she tell Mac of the incident. She hoped that the stranger would never come back and the incident worried her deeply.

Mac watched as Melissa drove down the path and kept looking until she went out of sight. He liked Mel, as he nicknamed her. She was bubbly, outgoing, and lively. She had brightened a spot in his heart and he knew that he needed her, especially now! He had fought so many inner demons at times, she helped him to cope. Mac walked slowly as he pondered things, he realized that she had the perfect balance of salesmanship with detail oriented structure. All of it with her personality and that was why she did so well selling real estate. Mac finally reached the corrals and brushed down the horses, and then left them to feed in the nearby pasture. He then saw to it the cattle were safe and did a walk around the Ranch, he took his rifle on these patrols. He will move all the animals to a nearby ranch near where Melissa lives when the season changes. He has an agreement with a friend who has a ranch to let his small band of animals stay there until the next summer.

Mac looked over against the ridge as the sun went down and soon the chill of the high mountain Wyoming air brought him inside. He made a fire and turned on the lights, sitting in his chair; he watched the fire and soon it got hot and the logs began to crackle. Outside he heard a howl of a coyote.

After a cold beer, Mac again took another turn outside, just like the Marshall's of the old west, who used to take one last look around town before night time and bed. He had to be careful. You would not know it, but Mac was well able to defend himself and he was an expert marksman with almost any handgun or rifle. He had spent tours in the Marines, and later in black ops overseas. Then he worked for private corporations in security before the Colonel got ahold of him. The only one meaner and tougher than Mac was the Colonel. Mac was sure in a straight on fighting match, he could beat the Colonel, but no one does that. Meet the Colonel one on one, that is. Most never see him or know he exists.

Mac got his infrared nighttime binoculars out of the case and looked outside. He thought he heard something, but nothing was there except some deer. He went outside and trod quickly to the edge of the forest that hid his cabin. Behind a large Pine, he saw lights. He quickly took the glasses and there were two black four-wheel drive vehicles with lights off, going slowly on the road past him. They stopped and got out; seems they were now discussing things. Through the glasses Mac recognized one of them. Sure enough, they were from the Colonel. These guys were snoopy, and their clearance was beyond black ops. These guys are so secretive that there is no trail to them. Just like Mac, they do not exist. Soon, though they all got in and headed down the road. It may be just time before they find the place Mac was at. They don't know his real name, have his location, or anything like that; but they are dangerous and too close for comfort.

Mac went inside and felt strange. His heart was racing. It never bothered him before, but now that he has left the Colonel and mind you; no one leaves the Colonel, for once in his life the feeling is strange. He seemed to be nervous, bothered, and a little scared. Could it be? Could he be having feelings for once in his long career? He has felt normal and free for these years since he has left. But now in the wide-open spaces of Wyoming trouble comes calling and so does his past!

As Mac came inside the fire was dying down and he threw another log on the fire. As he sat down, his phone rang.

"Mac" …you there; a voice yelled anxiously

"Tiger, little buddy" answered Mac; it was his nephew Billy and had just graduated not too long ago.

"I have not heard from you in a long time, how is your mom doing?"

"Fine, and remember she is not just my mom, but your sister; don't be so distant Mac", answered Tiger

"Just habit, so okay, now that you found me, out with it." Mac answered, "how is your mom doing?"

"She is fine, doing great in fact", she tells me to never let her know if I am hacking or if I hear from you. She wants to stay ignorant of it all, that way she can tell anyone interested that she simply doesn't know and not be lying." answered Tiger as he felt a bead of sweat on his brow

"Tiger, what have you done now; the only time you call is if you get in trouble" said Mac stressing himself, but Mac knew his Nephew; he was an adventurous sort, an expert hacker, and very snoopy. If you tell him to stay out of it, sure enough he will get into it out of sheer curiosity.

"I did it Mac, I did it"

"What did you do?"

"Curiosity Mac, plain curiosity that is what happened. I had gotten a job to get a little closer to a restricted facility I came across one day in the desert. All I had to do was deliver special messages and keep quiet. You think I can do that, keep quiet; well not on your life. This was a government contractor I worked for. So, when I saw the place, it was even stranger than I first thought. Then I saw the creepy Officer answer the door, which after getting the message, gave me a fifty tip and told me to scram. There was one main office and few outbuildings Mac, a barbed fence, and a guard post, surrounded by fifty some acres in all directions. Later I found out from my boss it was a secretive government project and get this an underground base. It was simply too Strange Mac! I went home to investigate it and see if I could find it on the internet. I did find it Mac, not the underground base; but the server which they use, that is one of them; I am sure they have many more. But I hacked it. That's when I crashed the server. But before it went dark, I turned up something called Project Black light; they know it was me, my identifying protocol. I saw the tracer's. I worked to hide my tracks, but you know, it is bigger than people let on. The project is underground, Mac, totally under the earth!" admitted Tiger

"You what, I have told you how many times to stay away from those things. All such projects kill people just for being too snoopy. They get away with it as well." Mac finished and was interrupted by Tiger.

"I know, Mac, I know you have warned me. But Mac, this guy; the officer I saw, get this! He was about 6 feet tall, had brown hair, well-groomed and had a mustache, like Hitler; you know the pictures of Hitler, well if he was not so tall; this guy would have been a spitting image of him." Tiger finished, his voice weakening.

Mac suddenly became frightened for his nephew; he knew who Tiger had seen. This person was none other than the Colonel and he is no one to mess with. He did not want to frighten Tiger, so he did not let on whom the man was Tiger saw. Mac listened as he heard Tiger breathing hard, he could sense the fright; then he said "Tiger you sound scared, frightened, do you realize what you have done. If you crashed this guy's place by accident or on purpose then, well does the word fish food mean anything to you."

Mac's voice stopped, and then softly continued "Tiger you will be okay just pack some gear and come meet me in Cheyenne. You have been here many times before, if you don't see me, then get going to the summer ranch; you know the one!"

"Yes Mac, I love that place; will do. I will meet with you in about fifteen hours and I won't stop for anything except a quick shot of gas and a snack." Tiger was calming down, he trusted his Uncle.

"Good Tiger, I will meet you on the interstate, going north just out of Cheyenne. When you get to the airbase look for my truck, you know the one. It will be parked off to the side, pull over and you can follow us to the Ranch." Mac finished, thinking and mulling over what Tiger said, "Project Black Light."

"Tiger the place where you were at, that could only the Alpha base. It used to be the old Project Orion black project. I will tell you more when you get here. We are secured here, both phone and internet!"

"Mac, hear me; nothing is totally secure, if you have a line, then it can be hacked; I know; I can hack anything, it's a talent, I can do this in my sleep. Now I wished I never knew how to do any of this." Tiger sounded tired and worried, Mac listened and then turned for a moment looking out the window.

"I know you're worried, but you can make in in a long day, say 14-15 hours. Don't worry we will give you more time. We will wait for you Tiger! Now be sure to take I 25 from Denver don't take any detours, stay on the Interstate all the way, you will make it Tiger, I have given you extra time, to be in Cheyenne. If you do not arrive, then I will take it they got you, but Tiger; I will come for you, I will find you! You can be sure of that!" Mac finished

"And another thing Tiger I don't think they really know who you are yet? You have some time, use that time to get here, so we can get ready for them. They will indeed find out Tiger, they will come sooner or later."

Tiger Gulped hard, "Really, how are you so sure of all this?" Tiger had packed and already made up his mind to go find his uncle, so by now he turned onto the turnpike and made his way north for Denver. He had called Mac using his cell as he drove out of town. He waited for Mac to answer him.

"Because if they knew who you really were; then you would be really dead! These guys do not mess around and they are the best at what they do and that is being secretive and killing people in cold blood, while making it look like a suicide. Need I say anymore?" Mac finished

"And Tiger, remember if we miss each other at Cheyenne, or if you're held up in any way then call me and leave a message. If you can't do that, then go to the Summer Ranch as I said before. Also, you can find Cliff's place, his name is on the mail box as you go to the ranch, and he lives some miles from me. You know Cliff, he can be trusted, you also can go there if need be." Mac paused making sure Tiger understood.

"Yes Mac, I know Cliff, nice guy and if I miss you; I will go to the Ranch!" Tiger stopped and took a deep breath, and then let it out. His voice sounded excited and cautious.

"Now don't worry, do as I told you, I will see you in Cheyenne and don't forget the truck you last saw me driving."

"Okay Mac, I will see you soon and yes I know the truck, the camouflaged four door Dodge truck with four-wheel drive and huge tires." Tiger stopped

"Yes, Tiger that is the one, see you soon, be careful." Mac put the phone down and got a stiff drink, sitting down he quietly watched the fire and listened to the sounds of the Mountain at night. As he sat there, the darkness and doom of something evil seemed to come over

him; reminding him why he left the Colonel in the first place.

Chapter Two: Secrets

Shall not God search this out? for he knoweth the secrets of the

heart. Psalms 44:21

"There are indeed many who believe now" the voice sounded

excited.

"Really, among the tribe?" was the reply.

"Yes, he has helped many to believe". Again, the voice was now

stronger emphasizing it.

"Listen Tom I don't know about all this stuff, are you talking about a

real-life Prophet. His voice sounding unsure, I mean like the Old

Testament stuff"

"Yes, my family has told me of the stories since I was a kid; passed

down from my great great grandfather who was a Shoshone 'newe

pohakanten' "

"A what?"

"Newe pohakanten, a shaman or medicine man to you. He lived in

the way of the 'mukua' or 'spirit' and the people knew he had great

'poha', that is power." Tom stopped and looked around. His place

was on the little Wind River and now you could see the cottonwoods
lining it and with the sun shining through. It looked so peaceful.
"What you are saying is there is a real life Jewish prophet
somewhere around here? That this guy comes and goes as the wind?
What is he doing here and why?

"Listen Todd, the people here, both Shoshones and Arapahoe's have
seen this guy. They speak of him having great 'Supernatural power',
he is one of 'nanishundehai', that is prayer, he lives among the
spirits and walks as the unseen. There are some who are fearful of
him." He did not tell him that he knew the Prophet and had been in
touch with him. The many stories about him were just that; stories.
But no doubt, he was a real life Jewish prophet and the Indians
around here respected him. He had come and healed many of their
people when they were sick. He was a respected one among the
tribe. No one would let on who he was or where he was living. But
he did know of the stories of such a Prophet that went back many
decades. He did not know if it was him, but he knew this Prophet,
for he had come late one night as he had been praying for his own
uncle to be healed and delivered. In prayer, he was interrupted by
the Prophet who came to their house. His uncle was healed and it

became a sign to the whole family of the real Prophet of God among them. He went on as he looked at Todd saying; "Stories in these parts go way back on this guy, some even claim to have seen him in the 1800's, but that is impossible. How can he be that old?"

"Well Tom, no doubt you sound serious enough, I believe you, and I don't believe as a Christian that you would lie. I know some in the group have mentioned him. But I know of no one who has seen him." Todd took in a deep breath as a breeze blew in the opened window. "Smell that air, love that fresh Wyoming Air".

Tom smiled at his friend, knowing the secret; he could not let on that he knew the Prophet, not just yet! Then he looks at Todd and said; "Yes, I love this country. Come on; let's go we have some stuff to do before heading to the meeting that is coming up"

"Right, let us go"

Tiger was on the interstate heading north on I 25. He had just passed the state line and entered Wyoming. It had been a long drive, but he was glad to have gotten this far away from those in Arizona. As he drove, the evening across the plains was blossoming into a great landscape for the antelope to graze and as he made his way past a large herd, he noticed something in his rearview mirror. There was a faint light in the distance and as he watched it, he also was looking at the road ahead. But he could clearly see a series of red and blue lights flashing. It came closer and closer so as it did, Tiger looked at his speedometer and he was doing 65. That's good he thought "I am under the speed limit". But the car pulled right up behind him and did not go around. Suddenly Tiger felt hot, sick on the inside and butterflies were doing flip flops in this stomach. Tiger slowed down and pulled over to the left along the road. He was now just out of Cheyenne and traffic was coming in all directions and everyone would glance over and then keep going. As he rolled down his window an officer came out of the car and walked up slowly. He was smiling and said, "did you know you were doing 85 back there!" Tiger look surprised, "85, but I was only doing 65!"

The officer said, "No young man, you calling me a liar? Now get out your driver's license"

Tiger fumbled for his wallet then he realized it was packed in his briefcase in the back. "Let me get it officer, I put it in my briefcase" "Certainly, young man, go ahead" The officer backed up and as Tiger got out, he turned to grab the briefcase laying on the backseat. Then Tiger noticed a man in the officer's car. He was not in uniform.

Suddenly he felt something in his back. "Well what do we have here", Tiger felt something point against his back, and it was a pistol.

Tiger jumped up suddenly and bumped his head lightly on the rim of the car. "What's the matter officer?"

"You know young man, we don't take kindly to snoops trashing our websites and computers", the officer was now wearing a wide grin and the man got out of the officer's car. The lights were now shut off and they were both closely surrounding Tiger.

Tiger moved a little to try to see the highway and let people know he was in trouble. Then he heard a car drive up. It slowed down, and a voice yelled out "Everything all right"

"Yes Sir, we are taking care of it, now don't block traffic and keep going or I will give you a ticket" The officer now looked at Tiger saying, "we finally caught up with you, after all; did you really think we would just let you go?"

Tiger looked at both now and meekly smiled and said, "I don't know what you are talking about; I am just a college student and heading back to the dorm right now."

"College, eh!" The officer laughed as he looked at Tiger, then he said, "take this car and go dump it, I will follow you with the body." The officer looked at his other partner who nodded and took the car on ahead. He knew he had scared the kid which was wanted he wanted to do. Fear was all over the kids face and now he knew it would not take much to make him talk. The Colonel had already nailed this kid when he first met him. They had a dossier on him, including his uncle known as "Mac". They knew it all and the real target was Mac, not this dumb kid who stumbled onto the website. It was sheer luck that he hit the site and just happened to be related to the one which they all had been looking for. They had been behind him all along waiting for him to make a move. Now with a little prodding, this kid would talk. He could always kill him later, but that was not on the agenda right now!

"Body" Tiger was now almost paralyzed with fear and as he moved a bit, suddenly the officer screamed as a car came careening into him. As it did, the gun fired, Tiger felt a sharp pain and dropped immediately.

Soon he was on the ground semi-conscious and could see two men get out and come towards him. They were talking about something. Then everything went blank.

Mac now was in place and it had been a couple of hours since he had been standing there. It was way past time for Tiger to have shown up. He looked over to another man standing there," what time do you have?"

The other man checked his watch and with a troubled voice said, "It is half past seven and well beyond my dinner time Mac."

"It is too long, too long" Mac now knew that something had happened to Tiger. If only his inquisitive nephew would stay out of things. From a child, Mac would sit down and relate wild stories of spies and secrets. Tiger always loved the stories and sis loved the fact that Mac would seem to truly love little Tiger. Which Mac did, he loved him. He was his only nephew and son to his only sister. But in his line of work, family was on the QT. You kept it quiet to everyone around you. So, all of Mac's contacts did not know that he really had a nephew or a sister and the ones helping him now were long acquainted trusted friends who in a spot of trouble knew how to kill, steal, and go under cover or do whatever was needed. They had worked alongside him in war, civil wars, political agendas, black op projects and now were helping him ferry this kid to safety. A kid that Mac told them was a friend's son and certain thugs had been threatening him. They did not know that Tiger had dealt a hand with the Colonel. Now it looks like the Colonel stacked the deck. Tiger was missing and Mac felt responsible for not doing more. But what could he have done? Nevertheless, he knew better! He knew the Colonel! Mac then knew that whatever it took, he would get the kid back, or if it was too late; he would kill the Colonel himself. He made this promise as he cranked up his truck and headed back on the interstate. He would head south to Denver and look for his car and a sign of what could have happened.

"Looks like the bullet went clean through, missed any vitals, here this will stop the bleeding" the voice stopped and looked around. Cars were still going by, some watching but as is the case today, no one wants to stop.

"Good thing we came by. How far are we from the Rev?" the voice questioned

"Not too far, it just out of Cheyenne past the truck stop going west towards Laramie. We can get him there. Where is the other guy?"

"Well he went ahead and it doesn't look like he saw us, or maybe he did and did not want to come back" the voice trailed off slowly.

Tiger could barely make out the words, they were muffled, he was in pain, and he was going in and out of consciousness.

"He is going into shock; let's get him covered up and in the back seat" One of the men moving to cover up the kid they rescued turned to his pal and said, "What about the car?"

"Leave it" replied the other man who was driving, then explaining himself he went on to say; "The Police can deal with it and I am sure they already know one of their cars have been stolen. They probably killed the Patrolman and put him in the trunk. So, let's get out of here."

 Soon Tiger and his two rescuers were on the interstate heading north; they came to the intersection and turned off on I 80 going west. It would only be about an hour or so before they would reach safety. Meanwhile, they had to keep this young man from bleeding to death. As they went, they prayed "Oh Lord forgive us for hitting that man, but he was going to kill this young man. Please Lord, heal this young man and keep him alive. Let us find out to whom he belongs and what trouble he is in so we can help him and deliver him from darkness.

What Tiger did not know and neither did those who sped by, that what happened was the result of two people being in the right place at the right time. It was not just mere chance and the two men knew it was a God appointment to make sure they were there when these two thugs were in the process of nabbing this young kid.

Now they were back on the road and going to the meeting of the group, a common term for a not so common people who were known as the Remnant. They were people who were not merely born again Christians but ones who had already taken a martyrs oath and were prepared to die. They would defend life to keep life alive. That means if they come upon people like they did today and see they were going to kill him, well then, they were committed to intervening; even at the point of death. Their numbers were growing and already many have died.

"You know I did recognize the one in the passenger area of the police car back there" said Bruce, the older of the two who was driving. Bruce had worked in undercover black operations for various departments in the government not to mention the military.

He had been to many of the hotspots in the world and was well traveled. He was dangerous in his own right and knew the tricks of the trade. What is more, he had worked with or fought against many who now were in the Colonel's secret core of killers. "That is why I first slowed down and asked the other officer if he needed help, I was ready to shoot. I saw his eyes, though, the look of a cold-blooded killer. I had seen his eyes before, a very long time ago, eyes that a person will not forget. That is why I turned around and came back."

"I know you knew him, when I saw your face! As for the other guy, well that was intense man, you really mean business. There for a second I thought you were going to shoot." Said Paul, a former pro wrestler and now working in the Remnant. Paul was well built, and with a lot of muscle. He was one you did not mess with, but Paul was born again and his real strength was the Lord. He was busy reading his bible.

"I would have Paul if I had not known the Lord. There would have been a day I would have killed them both with my bare hands if I could. They both are killers; they worked for a drug cartel back in the 90's. When I was working the border area in Mexico, I had a contract to hit many of them. These two I knew spot on, I knew the other one by name, his name is Carlos; The other one I only knew through the target scope when I was doing the contract those many years ago. I saw his face, then his eyes which had a look of pure hatred, cold blooded killer; that is what they said to me. It is a wonder they simply did not just shoot this young man and keep going."

"Do you think they will follow us?"

"Well if the other one spotted us, then he will come with reinforcements. He is a deadly killer. I heard though that there were many like him who are working for the, and get this; the "Colonel". Can you believe that? But make no mistake; it was the Lord who set our appointment to rescue this kid. I don't know who he is or what the Lord has in store for him, but this whole deal is not done; not by a long shot and If I know the Colonel he won't give up either!"

With that, the car fell silent as they moved toward their next stop at the Reverends. They both felt a sense of duty to the cause and right now they proceeded with purpose, salted with caution.

Early the next morning the smell of bacon frying wafted through the house and made its way to Gin's apartment in the basement. She rented the bottom apartment from her mother. It helped her mother out; now that Dad had passed. The arrangement allowed Gin to have privacy and keep track of her mother. She turned as the sun broke through the ground floor window and hit her in the eyes. The curtain was slightly askew and Gin got up and closed it tightly. She indeed liked her privacy but it was not like anyone could sneak up. Her mother had a big 8-foot-tall redwood privacy fence all around the backyard and the front had huge bushes and flower beds that prevented anyone from getting to close and eyeing in windows. Besides two huge German shepherds, Pa and Ma as they called them; had the back yard. The duo Shepherds had many litters of puppies over the years. Gin's family had raised them and sold them but now Pa was old and they neutered him when Dad died so they would not have to worry about puppies. But the two of them did not like outsiders of any sorts and kept the back yard devoid of strangers, cats, birds, and squirrels.

Gin was up early and took a shower; and then she made her way to her bedroom, got dressed and grabbed her pack. She had to leave again. The meeting of the Remnant was to begin soon, so she was preparing to leave again. She had to meet the Reverend about the meeting in Jackson she had and give him the information. After a short breakfast of fruit and a muffin; she was on the road. She would head south on I 25 to Casper, then to Douglas, and take the Laramie cut off and then hit I 80 and head east. That was the quickest way.

Things had not gone well. Now as he stood in a horse pasture somewhere in only God knows where, he was being yelled at by the Colonel. One thing about the Colonel, you don't do things badly. The fact that he is a cold-blooded killer an assassin only makes him worth more to the Colonel.

"How could you two of bungled such a job? I mean you both are professionals." Screamed the Colonel

"But sir, I went on ahead to the rendezvous, he was to follow right behind me with the kid's car. How were we to know that he would get hit by a couple of guys? He looked over at his partner whom he had gone back to get. He had a broken leg and fractured hip, he thought. He was in pain, but would live.

He looked around for any sign of cars and was relieved to see he was alone on this side road. The Colonel was heard breathing hard over the phone and he knew his boss was mad as hell, so he spoke up again; "But this no accidental meeting Colonel and these guys were not amateurs. They got the job done and were out of sight before you knew it. Someone must have known we were following him." The man finished now, satisfied that this would peak the Colonels interest.

"Not amateurs, very interesting and you believe they were actual professionals like yourself?" The Colonel became deeply lost in thought wondering if they had a mole inside. Did you recognize them from somewhere else, maybe from your last assignment in Columbia, or the towns along the border in Mexico?

"I did not see them, but Carlos says he thought he recognized the one who drove the car and hit him, but he is not sure". The man stopped and knew this would not suffice the Colonel who by now was mad as hell.

"Now get out and find this kid, I don't want him dead before I know what he wanted, who he is with, and where he was going. If we have a mole, then I also want to know if this kid has anything to say. But most of all, this kid is related to "Mac", he is the goal! You two get him, or start looking for another job, that is, if I don't have you both killed!" Now go find him or you both will be lying in a ditch with a bullet. I already have someone in waiting with a bullet that has your name on it. So don't screw this up."

The man stood there as he got an earful, the chewing out they got was okay for them both. They were valuable to the Colonel and so much so, the Colonel would not kill them; unless it was something bad. If the Colonel doesn't yell at you, then you worry! It is then; the contract on you has already been issued. That is the way it was and they lived with it. They also got paid well, very well; in fact, they both lived a lifestyle that only few people could enjoy. That is why they did what they did and did it for the Colonel. The money was good and so were the benefits. He hung up the phone, as the conversation ended suddenly with the Colonels typical slamming down of the phone hard to emphasize his point. As he stood there, he looked up and saw a strange figure on the horizon. The figure had the evening sun to his back, which made him a shadow. He could not tell who he was, but there he was. He reached for binoculars and as he scanned the horizon, the shadow figure was gone.

The lone dirt road went about a quarter of mile winding through two fields, one of corn the other wheat and led up to the big old farmhouse. There was a smaller white house off to the right as you drove into the main area of the farm. Up in front of the drive stood a big house had a huge screened in porch and a smaller front yard with a fence. To the left you could see a barn, the corrals, a few scattered out buildings, and implements of all kinds in the pastures beyond the house. There was a large hardened dirt road that made its way around the farm houses and corrals, with plenty of room behind the buildings for parking. It made it rather secure from prying eyes. Trees covered most of the property. It was nature's way to provide cover and privacy under the canopy of the cottonwoods which surrounded the main farm house and outbuildings. As a result, both drones and satellites could not penetrate the place, thus leaving them secure from prying eyes. A mail box at the entrance had the name of Schmidt. It was a direct play on words, because the ones living here knew Colonel Schmidt and he was the enemy who they fought. The real property owner was an anonymous person that for all intents was untraceable. Though, the Rev had lived here for more years than he could count his neighbors around him never asked questions. He was a farmer, which was just what the Reverend and his people did. They farmed, planted, harvested, and put up food. They bought and sold animals, and were in the biz of farming. This was the cover, one which had held up for many years.

Furthermore, it was also a matter of security to make sure that everyone in the group who attended the meetings knew the rules. They were to come in the evening or early morning if possible and not in multiple cars. Because of this arrangement, the neighbors were not aware of the things really going on there. Yes, there were people who visited with them, but nothing out of the ordinary.

Inside the fire was going as in the evening it would take the chill off the old house. Warming the bones as the Rev would say. In one corner amidst a huge office desk were two computers with several large screens attached. It looked like a news room. You could see a radio and transmitter off to the right next to the large file cabinet sitting there. The desk was a mess and behind the mess, with a green banker's light going; was the Rev. People called him that. The Rev was a fourth-generation minister and his roots went back to men of his family fighting with Teddy Roosevelt, in the War Between the States, and also in the Revolutionary war. He had been an ordained minister of the non-denominational type. But after he really got saved, as he says it, he quit and did the job the Lord wanted him to do. The Rev had a PHD in Theology and also was an avid researcher with a specialty in UFO's and related phenomenon; he was always busy on a project. He had been tracking the presence of the Nephilim which were seen around the country. In particular were two, no one knew their names. But they were very, very tall, some seven feet to eight feet tall, white, and well-built with blonde hair and blue eyes, but no pupils in them. As he was reviewing the latest reports from his website, a voice interrupted him.

"He is awake now Rev" called a voice, it was his wife Cynthia. She was a petite woman with dark brown natural curly hair. She was busy all the time with the house and its guests. She was one who everyone loved. The Rev called her the nice one. The Rev, however; could be grumpy and not so nice. He didn't like to be bugged when on a project. But the two, Cynthia and the Rev worked well together. She not only was the nice one, but meticulous and was always picking up on some finer points in their work which the Rev had somehow let slip. He was nice, but could not outshine his wife on this. Hers was a natural outgoing spirit. He was not outgoing and many times wanted to be alone. It was true that as a scholar and a leader, he knew the bible. He used that time alone to seek the Lord write, prepare sermons, and do research. He needed the quiet solitude and many times would wander off just to be alone with the Lord. He also was one of the very few ministers who knew the Prophet by name. They had known each other for many years.

The Rev had been working on some notes for the upcoming meeting and looked up, saw his wife Cynthia looking at him as if to say, "hurry up". Standing up, he looked lovingly to his wife saying; "Thanks I will go in and see him in a minute", and then the Rev after a moment of adjusting some papers he had been working on went to the guest room.

"Hello young man", The Rev said looking at a very young man who still looked sore. This had been the first time since he arrived that he was awake enough to say a thing.

"Hello" replied a weak voice. Tiger looked up and saw an older man with neatly trimmed beard, grey sideburns with salt and pepper hair. He looked over the man's face which seemed to exude wisdom and the man now had a smile broadening to a grin and brown eyes looking at him. He stood tall over the bed and saw a collar around his neck which indicated the man was clergy. Tiger looked with curiosity and wondered how he got here, but got lost in thought as he stared at the man's collar.

"You are looking at my collar, well young man; I just wear it sometimes to make sure where I came from. You see I had to get out of the ministry to find the Lord. Rather, he found me! Like the Apostle Paul I did things ignorantly and God had mercy on me because of it. So today I wear this collar to remind myself it not by man's denominational creeds, names, or work that men are saved by. They are saved by the grace of God through Faith, and the work of the Holy Spirit. Being born again of the Spirit, young man, of the Spirit of God and not man; that was my lesson. Now, how are you doing really!

"I am sore, very sore; can't move my shoulder; I got a headache and I am tired along with being confused." Tiger finished and then added "Where am I"!

"What is your name young man, I am known as the Reverend; call me Rev for short and this is our place. Friends found you and brought you here, having saved you from someone who was trying to harm you!" The Rev finished and saw the grimacing of the young man.

"Looking at the Rev and clearly hurting he spoke softly "my name is Tiger and I want to thank you for your taking care of me!"

"I will have someone come in and give you something for the pain and the headache. Don't worry, your safe among friends, we will talk about all that very soon. Just know that you're safe." The Rev finished and smiled once more and began to leave the room.

"Sounds good, but where are the guys who stopped me" Tiger asked

The Rev stopped and turned around looking at Tiger, "We are not sure. The one who was hit by the car never got up, we don't know if he is dead or was just hurt, the other one had gone on ahead. Suffice it to say, both will have to answer to a very mean Colonel and then they will be back in force looking for you. But for now, you are safe!"

Tiger smiled briefly and felt at peace, "thank you sir for your help"

"Just call me Rev, everyone does and the woman you see about the house is my wife Cynthia. If you need anything just ask. By the way, a friend of ours was a corpsman in the Navy. He looked at your shoulder and gave you a shot. It is a clean wound, and will heal nicely. For some reason the guy who shot you missed, thank the Lord; we know why he missed. Young man you are certainly blessed, the Lord was looking over you on that day. The guy was a certified killer, blood thirsty, we know him, that is, of him and who he works for. Now go to sleep, have some rest, our meetings will start soon and we want you rested so you can join in." With that the Rev left.

Tiger looked around and saw a tray of juice, different kinds of homemade breads, jams, and some fruit. He grabbed a piece of bread, dabbed it with jam and began eating. It sure tasted good. He took a swig of orange juice and a woman entered.

"Good, you're eating. I will fix you some hot stuff when you're ready. You will probably need a little more rest. You like the Jam; it is our own home-grown currents that we made it with."

"Yes ma'am, it is great", Tiger looked at her and smiled. He liked the Rev, something about him and his honesty. He looked up and saw her flowered apron over a long skirt. She had curly brown hair and her hazel eyes sparkled as she looked at him. He liked her as well.

"Just call me Cynthia, or ma if you have a mind; as many do" Cynthia's energy and enthusiasm made Tiger smile back at her. She was contagious; he had never seen anyone so happy, full of life, and friendly. Tiger looked at her and said, "Okay Cynthia it will be", he felt at home in these stranger's home. A sudden shot of pain made him grimace and then he became sleepy.

Cynthia looked at the young man lying there, he was so young and now he was going to need nursing and get his strength back. The Lord saw fit to save this man from death and she wondered what lay ahead for him. What work would the Lord have him to do! But most of all, what would the Colonel have to do with this young man, he is so young and innocent?

Melissa had just finished showing some property. She had to do a closing on a home she sold already and her office called to let her know there were several callers looking for places. It had been busy and it was time for a break. Melissa went into the local diner for a cup of coffee and a fresh homemade cinnamon roll. She sat in the booth with a clear shot of the street and the sun was shining down. It felt good as she waited there. Soon a waitress came up and had a pot of coffee and a cup.

"Coffee Melissa?" the waitress asked smiling at her!

"Yes Betsy! And a roll, the cinnamon one"

"Got it! I will be right back" With that the waitress left and behind

the counter grabbed a roll, put a large slab of butter on and

microwaved it for 40 seconds. Soon she was back with the roll and a

side of icing along with a fork. "There you go Mel"

Melissa's blonde hair shone in the sunlight as she slowly stirred her

coffee with cream. When she came into the café, men watched her.

She was a well-known real estate agent in town, but also one of the

prettiest. She was available and many men had tried to woo her but

to no avail. Now she sat with one of her first loves. Fresh baked

pastry, yes; a first love but one she did not eat so often. Melissa

worked out as well as being very busy selling. She burned fat and

worked hard to do it. As she sat, the first bite made its way into her

mouth, as she ate it slowly, the taste of the butter with the icing and

cinnamon with the pastry rolled around in her mouth. It was a taste

sensation to her, she loved them. As she sat in the sunlight, she

noticed a car with two men in them. She had not seen them looking

her way and by the time she did see them, they seemed to be talking

to each other and not looking her way. But for some unknown

reason, she felt uneasy; maybe it was being around Mac. He is always looking out for someone or something. She laughed quietly to herself as she thought of Mac.

 "See there she is. That is the one I asked some time ago. I know she recognized the picture we have of him! She knew him and turned me away. I know people; I can tell when they are lying about something"

"Really, you should say, sometimes you know they are lying"

"But I also saw her come back from where we had been searching as well. This was some time after I asked her about him."

"Really, maybe we need to have chat with this young woman"

Melissa finished her roll and looked out the window and notice that the men and their car was nowhere to be seen. She was relieved and she let out a big "sigh" which came out of her mouth as the waitress came up to check on her.

"What's the matter Mel? You okay, the rolls are fine aren't they"?

Betsy looked at her, she had seen something, her face showed it. They had been best friends since High School and had shared many good times together and many secrets. But unlike Melissa, Betsy married her sweetheart out of college and they opened this café in town. They did very well, but kept it small and with that the ability to do most of the work themselves. They worked Six am to 3 pm Monday through Friday. Melissa wished she could just work those hours, but in her line of work, it was seven days a week, sometimes filled with very long hours.

"Melissa looked up and smiled, saying; "no really; I am fine", and then she added "I am just thinking of all the work yet to do!"

That was good enough for Betsy who reminded her; "Mel you need a vacation"

"Yep sure do", with that Melissa left a tip, paid the check, and went out the door; heading for home. She had to pick up some paper work she left there. She looked at her watch and it was getting on to eleven. The afternoon went without a hitch and Melissa got a closing done on a property, and then showed several properties. One looked as though it would go through; the people loved it. She pulled up to the driveway and hit the opener and drove into her two-car garage. She grabbed her stuff and went through the door in the kitchen. As she opened the door something seemed not right. Her poodle was nowhere around. She always met her at the door. Slowly Melissa walked into the kitchen and then closed the door. As she put down her stuff on the table, an arm grabbed her.

"Hey doll, you want to play? A hand grabbed her arm and another tore at her chest to grab her, but her blouse tore away revealing her lacy white bra. The guy looked at her bare breasts and then laughed in a gruff voice, and then shoved her towards the table"!

Mel screamed as the smell of tobacco made her cough and she tried to cover herself. She was now firmly under their control. She breathed hard, was frightened, and fought to keep tears away. She was not going to let these buffoons know she was fearful. She fought as they dragged her to a chair and with her kicking and screaming the two men taped her mouth shut.

"Here sit-down doll, you have to explain a few things just keep quiet and answer our questions and you be will okay"

With her hands and feet both taped now, she was securely fastened to the kitchen chair. She could see her poodle, which lay in a pool of blood in the corner.

"Love your dog, feisty little bitch but in the end, I won, he laughed and looked at her. He could see the terror in her eyes, which was what he wanted." That made them talk all the quicker.

Melissa could see the other one looking over her legs and carefully measuring her breasts. His eyes were like the devils, he looked clean through her. He was the worse of the two, Melissa now feared for her life. She tried to close her legs but they were firmly taped apart to the chair legs and the guy was now looking at her crotch.

"Hey man, let's get a quickie off this bitch", the man drooled the words out.

The other man, clearly in control grabbed him by the collar and slapped him hard. Listen you idiot, this is business, we are not here for that. You control yourself or you will be alongside her. I can't believe they sent you to help me; you're an out of control nutcase. I am a professional, I do my job and nothing; not even pretty girls or their looks, I mean nothing will stop me; you hear! Not even you! He was now breathing out slaughter and hatred. He was mad, but in control. He turned around calmly now and looked at Melissa.

"Now don't' worry. Listen doll, answer me and we won't have to do anything else to you. Answer quick and I will just forget and move on. All we want is answers.

"You know this guy, right?"

Melissa saw the picture and sure enough it was Mac. Melissa shook her head no! The man came to her and ripped off the tape which made her angry as it pulled on her skin. "Now keep your words minimal, just speak when you are spoken too and I won't have to go any further. Now you know this guy, right?"

Mel looked up and saw the other man had now backed off and clearly subservient to this guy. The guy in charge was very tall, muscular and had a mustache. His large hands now gesturing to the other man and then he whispered something to him. He immediately left.

"Nope, I told you the last time when you described him I did not know him"

A sharp slap came across her face and made her neck jerk.

"Now, let me ask again"

"You know this guy right, where is he at, just answer and I will let you go"

Melissa paused; she saw the other one returning with a large sack filled with something, he put it out of sight and came to join the other one. His right hand twitched a little as he grabbed what looked like a pistol. He was getting anxious; she did not like his look.

"NO, I do not know him!"

Melissa saw the other one as he grabbed the pistol and came at her. In a flash she was unconscious with blood dripping in a pool at the base of her chair. He had cold cocked her with his pistol. When she

awoke, the two were eating sandwiches and drinking a beer.

"Doll, you are awake, good. You see we can keep this up, but take a

good look."

Melissa looked at herself in a hand mirror and saw they had

bandaged where she had been hit. She saw the guy smile as she saw

looked over her black eye and red welt on her check from the first

blow before they hit her with the pistol.

"Doll the next one will leave you a few teeth short, after that; well

let's just say you better tell us. Better yet I will change my mind and

hand you over to my friend here. He would love to roll around with

you. But know this he is bloody, he likes blood and sex! And You

are the perfect kitten for him!"

Melissa still had no tape on her mouth and anger surged in her "Man

you two are crazy! You two are big Men, tough men, taking on a

woman half your size. You think you are mighty both in style and in

sex, but you both probably have never had a true woman and are

very inadequate yourselves. Come on you two Bastards' if you're

going to do it, get it over with! I hate the sight of you and I was

scared before, but now I am mad as hell. Yes, you can rape me, kill me, and do all kinds of things to me, but I do not know this guy! I have seen him around and that's all." Melissa was breathing hard and now the two men stared at her in unbelief. She was angry and now finished speaking; she noticed that her arms were numb as were her legs and these creeps had her all to themselves.

"Listen Doll, let's get this straight, we know you know Mac; Okay; we have to find him, what is he to you? Is he worth dying for? Just let us know if you know him and where he is at" The voice trailed off and the devil eyed one stopped and piercing eyes glared at her.

"Your time is about up"

Melissa stopped and knew she could not go on for much longer. She could lie, and send them off in another direction. Then she had a plan. "Please guys, untie my legs and arms, they are killing me; I will tell you what I know, but don't hurt me."

"Well that's more like it doll, I knew you were smarter than you look", the devil eyed one smiled

"I am a successful sales agent in Real Estate and I came across this weird guy some time ago and sold him some property in Montana where I had some contacts. I got a small percentage as a finder's fee, that's all. I don't know him, I know of him! I met him only a few times and that was all. Melissa then gave them the directions and hoped they would let her go. She was in a spot and she knew it. If only she was more careful maybe, but how.

"Well doll, it is time for us to go, it's been great"

The devil eyed one opened the door for his partner who was in charge and now walking through the door.

"What should we do with her?"

"Kill her, then burn the house; make it look like an accident! Kept it professional we are here to do a job and be quick I will be in the car."

As Melissa sat there the devil eyed one came up with his knife and pressed it to her throat as he grabbed a breast and ripped it out of her bra; then he fumbled at her pants and sunk his hand in her crotch as he slit her throat, the blood dripped and he let out a yell; he was satisfied!

Melissa never felt a thing beyond the sharp knife, as her life drained away she thought of Mac, not the creep who was killing her and molesting her. She loved Mac and in the last few moments hoped that one day in eternity they could be together, then as the last of her life blood drifted away; she sunk down and gave a last gasp.

He got the gas can and poured out the remains all over the body and in the room. He turned on all the gas and made sure the pilot lights were out. He then went to the door dropping some gas on some clothes and lit it. He shut the door and ran to the join his compatriot in murder. They were professionals and one called himself Satan and the other one Lucifer and they smiled at each other as they drove out of the neighborhood and towards the Montana line. A short distance out of town they heard a blast and soon smoke filtered its way upward. The evidence was destroyed, after all they were professionals.

But what these two professionals did not know was that they had been spotted and their car tag recorded and the description of both them and their car would be given to the authorities.

Mac had been driving all night and his companions were still searching for Tiger. He needed rest but had to get back to the ranch. He needed to get online and find answers. He needed to make calls. He needed to enter once again the world of super secrets; the dangerous world of the black ops biz.

The night was dark, no full moon and as he drove the mountains, car after car passed him. He drove, but thoughts of things gone by filled his mind. Before long he heard a honk and saw lights coming at him, his quick reflexes pulled the car back on the right side of the road. He thought "you fool! You're too tired to drive". Mac saw a place to turn off, which he did. He still had a way to go, but needed rest. He had spent lots of time going road by road, highway by highway, and stopping by to ask questions of people if they had seen Tiger. But nothing came of it, Tiger disappeared!

Mac turned off the car and let silence be his friend. It was his nature; he wanted to hear nature itself. It was his way to make sure that if anything out of the normal happened he would hear it. He knew how to listen in such a way as to know if people are around or following you. He grabbed his pistol in his pocket and readied himself for a nap. If anyone surprised him, well his magnum 357 would greet them.

Soon a loud phone ringing woke him up and he fumbled around, he grabbed for it and missed it. His sleepy efforts to answer phone having failed, he looked at his watch and saw he had been asleep for around five hours, it was now early morning. He looked at the phone and the number who called was Cliff, his neighbor who has a ranch nearby. Mac called Cliff back.

The phone rang and in his study an older gentleman, grabbed the phone, "Yes"

"Cliff"

"Mac; I am glad to reach you; did you find your Nephew?"

"No, we have been looking everywhere for 48 hours and nothing; it's as if he disappeared off the radar" Mac sounded puzzled and Cliff knew he must be tired; after all he has been at it for a long time.

"Is everything okay at the Ranch?" questioned Mac

"Yes, both with my spread and yours; I was by yours today as usual and fed the animals, but look; you have more troubles, my friend"

Mac now worried, asked quickly "What troubles?"

"Well I went into town for breakfast and, as is my custom I read the early morning newspaper; while I ate. It had a main story about a huge fire that nearly caught on fire an entire neighborhood, but they got it out before it could do more damage than just one house and a few smoldering walls on the houses next to it." Cliff stopped and wanted strength to tell his friend of Melissa, but waited for the words.

"What Cliff is that why you called me? Mac sounded annoyed

"It is just not that Mac, it is Melissa?" Cliff fought back the lump in

his throat, this was hard; he hated death, then he added "but Mac, it

was Mel's house!"

"No, it can't be, she wasn't in it was she!" Mac yelled out loud

 "Well the newspaper says that she died in the fire. The cause is

being investigated and the news spread around town like wildfire. It

was in the coffee shop at breakfast when I arrived, even the Sheriff

was there eating. He had been at Melissa's house all night with the

firemen. They got statements of witnesses, but get this Mac, talk

around town, you know the coffee shop, well she was seen in there

before her death. She was worried and saw something or someone

out the window. The waitress, you know Betsy, saw her. She swears

Mel had seen something that worried her, but would not let on. The

police have witnesses, two in fact who say they saw two men go into

the house and come out of it before the fire. They gave the police the

tag number and description both of the men and the car."

Mac was silent; he lost his voice and his will to speak. He thought of

Melissa and as he let the news sink in, he heard Cliff again.

"And Mac, personally my friends in the department say this looks

like a professional hit. The police will want to talk to you since you both were seeing each other! I got a call not too long ago from the Police, I am to go in and give a statement as to how I know Melissa and if I could give any more information. But they do not have the forensics finished on Melissa's body for any evidence plus they will be going through the house for evidence for some time." Cliff stopped and listened, it was quiet.

Mac was silent for a moment, grief overtook him as he spoke softly; "Melissa, my dear, dear one; what have they done to you?" Mac, looked up suddenly as a car passed by him, shaking him out of his grief. Suddenly he was mad, then he spoke angrily; "Listen Cliff; be careful, you know my background; you're the only one I can trust. These people got to my nephew as well; I have been looking for him. Now they found Melissa. If Melissa had seen them before and they asked for me, she said nothing. I did see some of the Colonel's men the other day up by our spreads. I know their methods, I know the Colonel, and I know they killed Melissa to get to me. The fire and the murder fit some of the Colonels men. I personally know of two guys who work together, they call themselves "Satan and Lucifer" and believe me, they are indeed what they say they are. I wanted to kill them for some things I knew they did but the Colonel stopped me. These guys are not motivated by sex, rape, or any other fallible trait like most men. But they do have a blood lust, they love to kill and torment their victim. These guys are professionals and nothing will stop them. They are cold blooded killers, no matter whether you are a beauty queen or not, your charms will not affect them. They will use your own charms against you to get the job done. When they get you, there is only one result, you are dead; period. Nothing, but nothing can buy you out of that fate. They do their jobs well. If these guys did this, I will find out and when I do, I will kill them and send them to Satan himself. I know the Colonel's men will be able to find the Ranch sometime, but I must go home and gather some stuff, and then I will leave. Can you take a horse, a gun, and binoculars and watch for me? If you see anyone by the spread, call me. But don't get too close, the Colonel's men are dangerous. I would not ask you Cliff, but I know your abilities and your background, you are the one to help me get the guys who did this to Melissa. The cops will never catch them."

"You know me Mac, I would just as soon shoot them myself, but I will just watch out for you, be safe my friend" with that Cliff hung up

As they passed by the mile marker telling them they were now approaching the place where they left their other car, the two men; Satan and Lucifer smiled at each other. They had a satisfied look and were happy to be heading toward Mac's location. They arrived at the old cabin near the lake and it was around seven am in the morning. There was no one around and they found a deep portion of the lake and drove the car over the edge into it and within moments it was submerged some twenty feet down. They would eventually find the car, but not before they were well out of the area. They grabbed the other vehicle and headed north, listening to Blood Rock from the Sixties as they drove. The windows were down and they were cruising a comfortable sixty-five and the music blasted out the windows so hard the antelope looked up to see who was going by and causing such a disturbance. As the car came closer to the animals, they sensed danger and not knowing really who was in the car, sprinted off into the high mountain desert to get away from it. In the spirit realm, the bloody demonic spirits who possessed the men accompanied the two known in the spirit realm as pseudonyms of their boss Satan, the names given to them for their work. They had earned the high honors given them by their boss. When anyone does such wickedness, there is a reward and Satan himself gives it to them. There are special privileges but to these two also is given a seared conscience which is sealed off to the truth or of goodness and has forgotten of the True Lord God who will destroy all such wickedness one day and those who persist in it.

Mac sat quietly in the car. He liked Melissa, no it was bordering on love; no it was love. Why did he not tell her? As he sat there, grief swept over him and a tear came, then another. Mac was still tired, his body ached, and his head hurt, everything in his being seemed to be affected by the news of Mel's death. He closed his eyes to take in the news and saw Melissa in his mind's eye. He opened his eyes and looked around and for an instant thought he saw her standing in front of the car. He had done so much, he had been a killer, a murderer, and was a hit man for black ops. He knew murder and death. He knew other women, but now his heart was torn to shreds, it was broken; he had not been in a relationship like this for more years than he could count. Now the one he loved was dead and he knew the one responsible, the Colonel. Sure others did the dirty work, but the Colonel pulls the strings.

Mac sat for nearly an hour weeping and mourning for Melissa. When he was done, the crying was over, he would not weep again, he would not mourn, he would regret. He was trained to take people out and if they want war, by the name of the devil himself he would bring a war so bad so terrible and so bloody the devil would be ashamed. Mac was mad, hell raising mad and he was going to kill them, kill them all if he could. If he died, so be it. If he went to hades in the process, so be it! But come hades or high water, he would finish what they started. "I will get even, I will kill that S.O.B. I will send him to HELL or I will die trying so help me GOD!" Mac swore vengeance then and there.

Mac started his car and turned out on the road. It was now nearly 6 am and he was going to be driving deliberate, and with a clear mind. He could not let vengeance fog his mind, although he swore to get even; it was the professional killer instinct in him that would do the job. It would be cold, clear, and he would collectively use all his strengths to bring these to justice who did this to Melissa. He would not allow anymore emotions to enter him, it was too dangerous. If a fella allowed emotions to govern him, he usually made a mistake. As Mac drove, his old feelings, training, and professional killer instinct started to grip him. He was no longer out for vengeance. It was a job, they were scum, and he was the scum remover. He had killed so many men in this way; more than he cared to remember and so many he lost track. This was the cost of being a black ops sniper in South America. He had somewhere lost his soul and humanity in all that bloodshed. It was Melissa and the Ranch along with his friend Cliff that brought him out of it. He was beginning to feel like a new man, but now no more. Everything seemed to be taken from him and now, with nothing to lose, he was again Mac, the black ops sniper, who is so deadly, his nickname was 'murder incorporated' so named after the enforcement arm of the American Mafia during the 30's to the 40's. His best client, you guessed it, the US government. If he had a lot of blood on his hands, then the American government has an untold amount on theirs.

Chapter Three: The Project

A land of darkness, as darkness itself; and of the shadow of death, without any order, and where the light is as darkness. Job 10:22

The coffee was done and Mac grabbed a cup for himself and Cliff. He had come to his friend's house late last night after the call about Melissa's death. Today he felt empty and although the morning was well on its way in the high country, he sat down in his chair opposite Cliff.

"I can't believe she is gone", Mac confessed and then took a swig of strong coffee

"I know Mac, it is indeed tough, I really like Mel; she was sweet, pretty, and had brains", Cliff looked over to the window as he spoke.

The corrals stood in the morning sun and the horses were quiet. Mac interrupted Cliff's morning musings to himself with a thump as he hit his fist on the counter.

"Why couldn't they just leave her out of it?" Mac said angrily

"Mac, you know these guys, they saw through something, suspected something. They must have thought Melissa had some info or maybe even asked her. The answer they got apparently did not go far enough. Somewhere though, is that little known reason of why they did what they did and why they are looking for you. 'Cliff finished and scooped up a piece of toast and egg on his plate and swallowed it.

"I know they will pay for what they did to her! But if they are still looking for me, by the God above that these guys don't believe in, they will find me and when they do, hell will come into their lives. "Mac stirred his eggs and potato's, looking at his breakfast he pushed it away. He did not feel like eating.

"It's the project Cliff, if only I had never been associated with that black project!" Mac admitted, then continuing he said "This project will be the death of America and not one soul outside of this black op project knows that fact! We must not only give due retribution for

Mel and Tiger, but we must stop this damnable project straight out of hell!"

Mac and Cliff suddenly heard Cliffs Australian Shepherd pair, Sun and Ray barking at something outside. Cliff went to the door and saw the two were chasing a squirrel that got to close to the food that had been put out for them. Cliff laughed and motion to Mac, "they found a squirrel, they never catch them, but it does give them exercise".

Mac looked up smiling, "you have got a great pair of dogs here Cliff, I would have some if I were not gone so much"

Cliff nodded and knew that with these two dogs, Sun and Ray nothing passed by or came close without them ushering a warning. They had been trained to keep strangers off the property and if they did find someone close they knew how to keep the intruder at bay. They also knew kill order on command. If in a firefight, both dogs would fight and die for Cliff and those with him. Cliff loved these two dogs immensely.

"Mac, I do have a present for you. I bought it some time ago. You will need what I have for you. I know you have your own, but I saw this one advertised on eBay. It is a M110 semi-automatic sniper rifle.

The ad says it chambers a 7.62x51mm NATO round; a 308 mag. I got the 20-round magazine, a suppressor, and a Leupold scope. I got extra ammo for it, a case, and packed it with care." Cliff finished, and then added "I thought some of your rifles may be a little outdated".

Cliff brought in a large wrapped box and handed it to Mac, adding "an early Birthday present"

Mac opened the box and saw the rifle, in short order he had put it all together and tried it on. The army cameo green exterior, clip of shells, stand, and scope felt good in his hands and reminded him of times gone by. It had been many years since he had shot anything as a sniper and he had hoped he would not have too, but in a fire fight, this would do fine.

Smiling, Mac said "thanks Cliff, I will go outside soon and do some shooting"

Cliff looked at Mac and the rifle, he knew full well this rifle could save his friends life and those around him. With those men around who killed Melissa, it is important to be prepared. Cliff grabbed his side holster and brought out his fifteen shot semi auto 45, looking at Mac he said "I am ready as well, my little gal here will get me out of a bind, but I do have heavier firepower. But truthfully, my old 30-06 is sweet as well. I have used her often to bring down Elk, Deer, and Antelope. Believe me; it will make a hole clean through anyone who causes trouble. I still have some armor piercing shells for it, those will come in handy."

Mac looked at Cliff and said "You need to stay out of it. I already lost Mel, Tiger is missing, and I don't want you involved in this."

"Well, I became involved the minute they killed Mel and took you on. Remember, bro; we are blood."

"I know, we have fought and worked together, much blood has brought us together, I understand this; but you don't know the Colonel like I do. I just don't want you hurt, or even killed" Mac finished and saw the argument was getting nowhere with Cliff.

"I can't hear you, not at all" with that Cliff began whistling and with a wry smile; went outside

Mac followed and took the gun, bullets, and grabbed some targets from the nearby table. It would be a morning of target practice.

The Colonel turned just a bit and saw the soldier standing at guard in the front of the staff meeting room at Alpha base. It was early morning, around 5 am and the Man as everyone calls him was visiting the base. Actually, the Man was Brigadier General Tommy Johnson who is over the South West Quadrant and Alpha base is one of four in his group. The Colonel oversees Alpha base but also provides a specialty service for the General as his right-hand man and clean-up specialist. It was always the Colonel who was the one that did what was necessary.

They were both eating a breakfast of Steak and eggs, with strong military grade coffee. The stronger the better and the longer it sat just made you either gulp it or take your time depending on the preference to get it over with. Yes, this was no Starbucks and the brass herewith was not here for the coffee or the food. This was the Project Black light Alpha base.

The general stopped eating for a moment, wiping his face, looked at the Colonel, paused again as if thinking and then spoke; "Colonel let me tell you a story. You know the current sitting President?"

"Yes, General" answered the Colonel

"Well long before he was President, I was stationed at another base, Project Black Light was just in the early stages and I was waiting for the final building to be finished. I was outside and discussing some things with other officers and we had just come out of a meeting.

Just then a long line of black limos pulled up, flanked by black Humvee's. Two sharply dressed men in black had stepped out of one of the Humvee's and came directly to me. They asked me to step into this long limo. As the door opened I could not see who was on the back seat, and they motioned me to sit on the other seat facing towards it. As I sat down, I saw him. He greeted me with "Good day General". It was the current President, but he had not been elected yet, what is more; it was years before he was to be elected. I had been told that all plans had been made at the highest levels for him to be elected. As I sat there, I looked directly at him and greeted him with a "Hello Mr. President"; to which he replied smiling "So you know I will be President" he asked. I said, "Yes sir I do".

"At the highest levels Colonel that is where our arm reaches. You and I are on the front lines and merely doing the bidding of people that have had this planned for many years. The public thinks they elect him. That is poppycock, we elect who we want; that is all there is to it. We have worked hard to 'steel' the darkness; that is to make it impervious to attacks. Just like solid steel, we must be hardened! As we have covered this land with our own people and thus increasing our power; we are nearing the day when this land will be ours and the darkness will be a 'steel' coating impervious to attack! Colonel can there be anything that could ever destroy what so many 'principalities and powers' have put in place?" The General stopped and took a drink of coffee and looked at the Colonel.

"Well general, there is one man who concerns us. We have been tracking him and found evidence of him in Wyoming. We believe some of his men are responsible for the server breach not too long ago. They were not able to get any info, but the system did crash and our techies are working to fix it now." Stopping, the Colonel remembered Mac

"Well who is the person you are talking about" The General asked

"Mac, known as 'Murder Incorporated', you may not know him; but he worked in many places in Black Ops. The last of his jobs was in South America and on the border of the USA. He alone is responsible for wiping out entire families of cartel leaders." The Colonel finished, "if anyone can literally assassinate anyone, it is Mac. He is bloody, very bloody and when he is on a mission even the devil is afraid".

"I have indeed heard of him. Too bad we can't enlist him." The General speaking, then he saw the eyes of the Colonel and suddenly, the General spoke again "What is it Colonel, what have you not told me?"

"General he was with us, but for some reason he left. No trace of him anywhere until just a few weeks ago. He knows who we are and what we are like and how we operate. I have ordered hits on him and nothing. It is like he vanished, that is until we got another lead these last few days. I have dispatched more hit teams to the area."

"Colonel, this is very distressing news. No one leaves us. Anyone who wants to leave does so in a pine box. You had better get this Mac and anyone with him. But Colonel, although you will have to kill him, you cannot let it be known it is murder, it must be an accident and must not be connected to us at all. We are very close to moving forward to phase 3 of the project. "The General finished and his anger showed on his face.

"Yes, I agree General and Yes we know the rules; he is a dead man", with this the Colonel grabbed his coffee and poured a shot of Tennessee walker red into it and did the same thing for the General, saying "General let us toast to it and to our success, to make sure we Steel the Darkness and ensure our Kingdom on earth."

The cups clinked together and both the Colonel and General looked at each other smiling, and then laughing out loud before they gulped down the drink. So loud you could hear the sinister shrill of their laughing in the hallway. It was enough to make people stop and wonder, what was going on.

The plots and plans were in gear and the General said his goodbyes leaving the Colonel and his staff to finish what must be done. The Colonel paused to make sure he was alone, and then thought to himself Mac would be killed, they would win! The Colonel moved to walk down the hall as he neared the door, he looked up and thought again; what he did not tell the General was Mac was no ordinary hit. He knew Mac would not be fooled like most people and if it meant a direct hit, they would do it. If it meant not looking like an accident, so be it. Mac was one of them and in a fight, there was no equal. He would be killed whether by accident or not, they could take no chances. But maybe there is a chance to turn him back to them and rejoin the team. Yes, that would be good also! With that the Colonel smiled quietly at the thought of Mac rejoining the team, but really, he knew that death was the only option with Mac. Mac was too dangerous and he knew if anyone could kill him, it would be

Mac! It would be safer and healthier for the Colonel if Mac died, as the Colonel stepped out into the hallway; his mind was made up, for his own good; Mac must die!

Gin had arrived at 2 am and now was drinking a hot cup of coffee and eating some toast and jam. It was 9 am and the Reverend's place was buzzing. This was Remnant central for the group. The meeting would go on as usual, but she had to come down and go over some things with the Rev as everyone called him. Cynthia, the Rev's wife was outside feeding the chickens and doing the necessary chores. Most of the group when they came bunked out in the other house, and outbuildings on the place. The group had eyes from various positions in all directions, out of sight. There were people among the group, former military who took turns at the watch. They used night vision glasses or strong binoculars during the day. There was a warning system that could be triggered by anyone in the group via the wireless controls. Nothing could escape the eye of the group and with the open fields, even with crops; there was a lot of open ground to cover before anyone got to the house. In case of a breach, there was an underground bunker and a passage that ran under the field which provided an emergency escape if needed.

"Hi Gin, did you get any sleep?" asked Cynthia as she came in from outside

"A little, enough though. I am doing fine with this coffee and toast. By the way your homemade bread is great, I just love all the whole grains you use in it." Smiling Gin looked up and saw the Rev come in from outside.

"Hi Gin" greeted the Rev as he grabbed a cup of coffee

"Hi Rev" answered Gin as she watched both the Rev and Cynthia pull up chairs at the table opposite her.

Cynthia had a newspaper and starting to browse she saw a story from Israel. She adjusted the paper and looked at the Rev and got his attention to what she was reading. "Say Rev, something is happening in Israel."

The Rev looked up, swallowing a piece of a roll; he took a swig of coffee, "Yes I saw it"

"Well what do you think? What are they up too!" asked Cynthia as she began reading the paper aloud, "Witnesses on the grounds of the Temple Mount and Jerusalem were all confirming the same story that a large contingent of silver craft, UFO's could be see over the Dome of the Rock itself. The craft were seen hovering over the

Dome for around five minutes and then were watched leaving the area. Some say the saucer shaped craft simply disappeared". Cynthia stopped and took a gulp of coffee, then continued "it was further reported by witnesses that globes of light in the hundreds also appeared at the Temple mount and various locations around Israel speculating that something supernatural was happening! Even more bazaar was the fact of others coming forward saying they saw tall humanoid like people walking around in Israel itself at the time of the sighting over the Mount. Witnesses say these were not human, but very tall human like creatures and had on some metallic like suit that fit them perfectly. In Israel many saw these events as supernatural signs and speculations of Gods, Nephilim of Genesis 6, or other Alien creatures were circulating Israel after this massive sighting."

"Cynthia stopped and saw Gin looking at her in unbelief while the Rev was simply smiling.

"These are part of the end of day's deception. Stories like that one has been circulated for some time. The witnesses are real, I am sure they are not lying. They saw something! In fact, there have been many UFO sightings in Israel. But there are those in Israel that see these visitors as heaven sent. They do not see them as a demonic or an evil presence, in fact they like them. We are seeing more and more sightings of UFO and other mysterious appearances all the time. The truth here is that no one has really seen an Alien or Nephilim in person! It is interesting; however those Israelites that saw some humanoid creature described it as tall and compared it to the Genesis 6 Nephilim. From Scripture we know they existed. We also Caleb and Joshua fought them in the Promise land and destroyed them. Some; however, seem to have escaped to other regions of the world."

"However, I believe all this can be connected to those like the Colonel. It is known that the government has been in contact with an Alien presence for decades. The Government gets Alien technology to use against their enemies to control the system. Then the Aliens get to be in the earth operating out of American black ops bases, all with the agreement of the United States Government" The Rev finished and began to ponder the events, as he did; Gin and Cynthia looked at him.

The Rev looked up and saw that both Cynthia and Gin appeared anxious at the news in the paper. "Don't worry you two, it will be alright! The Lord has never failed us and besides all of it will come together one day. We may not fully understand all aspects of it. The Nephilim are the 'sons of God', the fallen angels. UFO's are part of the end of day's deception and the Aliens are demons. We also know that the Lord has placed in his Word some enlightenment on this. If you do a search for the words delusions and delusion; you will only find two scriptures in the entire Word of God on it. Just two! The first is in Isaiah chapter 66 and verse 4, where the prophet speaks to Israel saying, 'I will also choose their delusions, and will bring their fears upon them; because when I called, none did answer; when I spake, they did not hear: but they did evil before mine eyes, and chose that in which I delighted not'. The other one is Second Thessalonians chapter two and verse eleven which says, 'and for this cause God shall send them strong delusion, that they should believe a lie'. From these we know that when a people like Israel, or even America, or other people refused to answer Gods call to repent and ignore him and those people continue to do evil in God's eye's doing those things he detests, then God responds in His Word with 'I will choose their delusions' and second 'I will bring their fears upon them.' The other scripture is found in context with another scripture that says in the end of days those people it says 'received not the love of the truth, that they might be saved, for this cause God shall send them strong delusion.' People even now reject Gods love and that of his Son who died for them. Most people know John 3:16 and it is the verse which tells us of the love of the truth. God so loved us that he sent his son whom he loved and his son so loved his Father and loved us that he came and died for our sins. This is the love of the truth and that which makes up the gospel of salvation. People in this end of days will reject it, they will not believe this truth, and they won't receive it so they might be able to be saved. Because of this, God then sends them a delusion, a strong delusion so powerful they will believe a lie. Both the Son of Perdition in Second Thessalonians and the Beast of Revelation chapter 13 form the basis for the end of day's deceptions. But Isaiah also tells us that God will 'choose their delusions' and bring 'their own fears upon them'. Today, UFO's, Aliens, and even the Nephilim make up that 'strong delusion', and also forms that which people are afraid of; here God 'brings their own fears upon them.' This delusion is so powerful people will believe a lie over the truth of God's love and salvation. This is the work of the devil and of men whose hearts are cold and their conscience seared; they love darkness more than the light. This is the battle we face today. But know this, Nephilim are real; a real viable entity and alive on earth today. Aliens per se, are demonic beings masquerading as something they are not, appearing as they wish. Now in saying this, know I based my statement of Nephilim on Genesis six. As for Aliens being demonic, unless I see some other scriptural and physical proof, and the Lord reveals the evidence of such; I am left with the conclusion. I am not in agreement with the Vatican on welcoming Aliens and baptizing them as the Pope has called for in the past!" The Rev stopped and gulped some coffee and pondered the events in the paper.

The Rev, Cynthia, and Gin sat quietly and a silence permeated the kitchen area where they were. Soon they began praying, and before long; others joined in and they all looked to the Lord their God and Father and Yeshua Ha Massiach; the only begotten Son of God. As they did, the Rev spoke up in earnestness as he did the others quieted down being used to the Rev leading important prayer over the group. "Father, the Rev prayed we seek thy face in the name of thy Son Jesus Christ; we thank you for your protection over us and keeping us. We thank you that you brought Tiger here safely but we know also the devil's henchmen sent from the Colonel are responsible.

But, Lord; most of all what would the Colonel who is so evil want

with this young man. Lord, he is so young and innocent? Today,

Father we are reminded of your word that Yeshua prayed for his

disciples in John seventeen; where he said, 'I pray not that thou

shouldest take them out of the world, but that thou shouldest keep

them from the evil'. I pray Father, we are in the world, we declare

thy love to this generation, therefore Lord keep thy Children; every

one of us from the evil, that evil one the devil and all his people and

powers; keep us Father in Jesus name" the voice of the Rev got

quieter and shouts of amen and praise the Lord were heard.

The group stood, some knelt, others continued praying while others

sang quietly; the choir of voices lifted the place into the heavenlies.

Soon, although the eye could not see them; angels moved quickly

among the members, touching them, blessing them, in the name of

their God whom they served. As this began to climax, the devils and

demons in the spirit realm were seen fleeing from the presence of the

uplifted voices and prayers being made. Surely, in this spirit realm at

this moment the supremacy of the Lord of Lords and King of Kings

who triumphed openly over all principalities and powers was

demonstrated. The group began to become quiet and they looked up; a supernatural calm and peace came upon the group and they felt the presence of the Lord and in their hearts, faith arose and they knew that whatever came upon them, the Lord would be there with them; of this they all were sure.

He looked at his watch, it was 4 am. All was quiet this early morning. Making the rounds the sentry made one last check and looked out over the secluded base and could see the Pacific waves in the glimmering pre-dawn. The Hawaiian foliage was all round Bravo base two one niner and it was this reason that many did not know much about this project of the US military. It was another black project and it housed the Weather modification defense systems known as WMODS. The sentry looked toward the main office building which now had some lights on and the DOD could be seen on the porch looking around. The labs and systems control bank were off to the left and had quarters adjacent for the scientists and technicians who made the system run. They all had above Top-Secret clearance and had no personal life at all. They ran, tested, and used ongoing weather modifications to help the US and her allies in the daily defense analogies.

The morning air was clean and fresh, you could literally taste the salt of the Pacific from where the Officer of the Day stood. The area seemed alive with all the birds and other animals, which in the early hour made it known, that they too, were awake. As the officer took one last drag of his smoke, the phone rang inside.

"Bravo Base, Lieutenant Anderson speaking, can I help you"

"Yes, you can Lieutenant, I am Colonel Schmidt is your C.O. in yet?"

"No sir, not for a while; he usually goes for a run right about now" answered the Duty officer quickly

The Colonel sounding irritated spoke "I need you guys to do a WMODS today at a location which marked, will be sent to you through usual channels. It is National Security and must be readied and acknowledge from your end ASAP. We have ongoing operations and must have your coordinated Weather modification in conjunction with our project. Do you understand me Lieutenant?" The Officer was used to such gruff and official voices addressing him, and he answered, "Yes Sir" with that, Colonel Schmidt said "Good Soldier" and then hung up.

In a short while the communications officer came out with a message, and told the DOD, "We have a secure code request for a WMODS, we have the location, date, and time; we will pass this on to the C.O. as he comes in." It would be the C.O. who verifies the message directly and then would send another secure coded confirm request to the one seeking the WMODS. This way, double confirmation would ensure no mistakes. After confirmation, it would be then assigned and prepared to be carried out.

The C.O. sat at his desk and read the request for the Weather medication and saw that it was coded for a place in Wyoming, in a couple of days. They were to have a small earthquake, followed by a severe rain storm. It only took about 45 minutes for the double confirmation to be verified. As was most of the requests, this one was a matter of a national emergency and so the C.O. rang up the Bravo base assignment task Officer and gave him all the information, with longitude and latitude. When it was in the system, the state of the art H.A.A.R.P. systems and computers which were linked with others would fire in the necessary time to bring the Weather modification to completion. It would look for all intents and purposes as an act of God. Only a small few actually believed the capabilities were there for the US black ops project WMODS to be able to do what they do. The project likes it that way. Even Washington does not know of what it does. It is entirely a black project and kept totally off the radar. The Alpha and Bravo bases are connected along with others to ensure the capability to govern and to bring in the current project Black Light and its agenda.

Tiger gingerly moved his body slowly and with help, was able to put on a shirt that one of the guys there gave him. He did not know who rescued him and many details of his encounter with the Colonels men were very vague. However, he was glad to be with the group he was with. They were nice people and the Rev and his wife Cynthia were great. Tiger really liked them. He finished dressing and went out into the main house, looking around he saw a few people reading. As he looked around he saw the kitchen with the Rev in view. He went over and saw that Cynthia along with another woman was there. She looked to be a little older than he, but she was good looking. As he moved into the kitchen he grabbed the last empty chair and sat down looking at the Rev.

"How you feeling young man" The Rev spoke calmly

"Tiger, er I mean my real name is Billy Ames, but everyone calls me Tiger, since we never were really formally introduced", he smiled, and then turned to see a good looking young woman smiling at him. She held out her hand and said;

"Glad to meet you Tiger, I'm Gin."

"Tiger we are glad you are doing fine; the Lord certainly has raised you up and given you strength." Cynthia added smiling, and then asked, "you want some coffee and a roll or something".

"Black coffee with cream and sugar plus a roll would hit the spot", then Tiger looked at the Rev asking him "how soon is that meeting you wanted me to be at?"

"In a few days, why?" asked the Rev

"Because I need to go get my Uncle Mac, at least tell him I am okay and where I am at. He is the kind to never give up and I can tell you he is looking for me; not to mention being worried. Worse yet, he probably blames himself for me disappearing." Tiger took the coffee that Cynthia just sat down and took a drink

"Where does your uncle live Tiger"? Asked Gin

"He lives on a Ranch north of here, close to Federal land, not too far from the Montana border. I used to visit him in the summer when he was free from his assignments. However, on the ranch with Mac it was hard work, but the perks of hiking, fishing, and hunting made up for it. It is hard to find; very secluded and on private land. Not many know of it because no one goes there unless invited. It belongs to a private company; you see!" answered Tiger as he saw the Rev take out a BLM map.

"Here is a map of that area, point it out will you Tiger" asked the Rev as he spread out the map.

"Here, right here off of the main road going north", Tiger stopped and looked around

"Man, what is your uncle the President", joked Gin, then she added "that is not too far from where I live!"

"No, but Mac is a former military and black ops specialist, and he is very special to me; plus he was more of a Father to me than anyone else." Tiger finished and looked at Gin.

"Are you part of this Group, what do you call it again Gin" asked Tiger

"Yes, Part of the Remnant, it has become very large since America has left off constitutional freedoms and taken in their global agenda. We have contacts all over America and places in government that no one would suspect." Gin finished, smiling she looked at Tiger, but then she asked "when do you want to leave? I can take you; the Rev and I have some things to go over before the meeting, so if I get back early that will be fine. You are coming back Tiger, aren't you? Asked Gin

"Yes, of course, I like it here and I also like your beliefs. I want to know more as to your faith and religion", Tiger answering Gin adjusted himself and looked at the Rev who was listening intently

"Tiger" the Rev said interrupting the conversation between the two, "are you thinking of leaving today?"

"Yes, Rev; the sooner I let Mac know I am okay the better; he will be at his ranch or maybe Cliff's"

"Well get ready Tiger, we will pack some food and drinks, but we will also send an extra couple of the group along to help you keep safe" said the Rev looking serious and adding "we know the Colonel will not give up, you must be very careful as his men will be watching all roads so go incognito. Our people will dress you differently and make you look like someone else. We are commanded in scripture to be 'wise as serpents and harmless as doves.' So that is what we do, try to outsmart them." The Rev finished and stood up, saying "I got to go stretch my legs and talk to the Lord, but don't leave without saying goodbye to me" with that the Rev left the room and went outside.

"Well it is settled then", said Gin "let's be ready in a couple of hours and then we can go"

After saying goodbye to the Rev, getting their disguises on; Gin and Tiger were ready to go. Tiger had his hair cut shorter, a new mustache, and a cowboy hat and boots on with Levis that were well worn. He looked like a Cowboy. Gin had readjusted her hair, making it look different and put on more western type clothes, got a different car, this time a new model SUV; and with them were two others from the group. It was the same ones who found Tiger, and both also had different looks to themselves. The pair introduced themselves to Tiger. These two were Bruce, a former black op's sniper and Paul, who had been a pro wrestler; both of whom looked formidable in a fight. These were the two who rescued Tiger. The two looked at Tiger and extended their hands.

"Thanks guys for saving me from the Colonel", Tiger greeting them as he reached out to shake Bruce's hand, but suddenly he was grabbed and given a solid hug; "glad you're better, and I am happy you are with us", with that Bruce finished and stood aside.

"Likewise, bro" said Paul, who shook hands and then ended up giving him a hug as well

Tiger smiled at them both as he moved his hand to get feeling back into it. Paul, the pro wrestler sure had a strong grip.

"Oh sorry about that Tiger, it's my wrestling, I do that without thinking; I have a strong grip" admitted Paul.

"That's Okay, I am glad you two are coming along", with that Tiger turned to go; Bruce and Paul following him.

As they left the Rev's; Tiger and Gin both felt comforted by the company of Bruce and Paul. Tiger liked the fact that the Rev prayed for him and also asked God to keep them all! In case they did run into the Colonels men, these two would be able to provide an extra layer of safety for them. Gin was now driving and turned onto I 80 going towards Laramie, then highway 30 to 287 and on to 220 to I 25 and then head north from there. They should be at Mac's in about five to six hours give or take driving time. Tiger settled back and closed his eyes while Gin seemed lost in her thoughts as she drove. Both Paul and Bruce were talking quietly and looking at the cars passing; checking every vehicle that came close to them. With the sun high in the sky and the heat of the Wyoming day pouring in through the window, Gin turned on some air and settled in for a drive to a place and to a meeting with someone she does not know. She hoped that they would be welcomed and that the Colonel would be nowhere around.

But as Gin drove, she seemed to feel in her spirit that trouble was brewing and they would run smack dab into it before the day was out. Somewhere evil was lurking and behind that evil were the devil's chief servants, the Colonel and his men. But then as these thoughts arose, she also knew that the Lord was with them and would deliver them out of all the hands of the wicked. She had seen time and again the Lords protective power over the group.

Mac and Cliff stood on the embankment overlooking the Ranch that Mac called home these past months. Sun and Ray were somewhat apart sniffing out tracks and strange smells. They were well adept to the Wyoming out of doors. They knew friendly creatures and knew what to stay away from, like a porcupine or a skunk. Cliff let them alone; they would never venture far from his side, wherever Cliff went the two dogs followed, it was that simple.

Sun had puppies not too long ago and all were sold. Cliff looked forward to a new batch of the little ones, this time he planned on keeping one.

All looked quiet, but they stood with rifles and glassed the entire area. They could see the highway from where they were and a few cars passed by. It was all quiet. Against the hill, the pines stood tall providing shelter for a large white tail deer that looked up as Mac glassed the area. The deer seemed to be looking at something, but Mac could not see what it was from his viewpoint. Within a few moments, though the Deer went back to grazing and all seemed fine. It must have been another animal, Mac thought.

Cliff went over and sat on a log nearby. He grabbed the thermos and got the two cups he and Mac were using. He filled them with hot coffee and walked to Mac.

"Here Mac, have a cup; see something there do you?" asked Cliff as Mac turned around and got his coffee out of Cliff's hand.

"No, just a large buck" Mac answered and took a sip of the hot liquid

"Do you think the Colonels men will find this place, I mean really? Maybe Mel did not tell them all of it." Cliff asked knowing the answer would be yes

"Well, I do indeed believe they will come, even if Mel did not tell them; they have a way of finding out everything. Personally, Cliff I want them to find this place because I have something to tell them and a message to give to the Colonel. If they do come, they had better be prepared to meet hell and death because I will bring both with me to meet them. There will be no mercy!" Mac finished, as he did; a chill ran down his back, he shivered; he was not Mac the rancher anymore; he was Murder Incorporated, a cold blooded lethal killer out for a pay back. "

Cliff understood this side of Mac and knew it would not go away until the job was finished. Many would die before this was over, but Cliff hoped that Mac could return to a normal life and to be a regular guy. He could get over Mel's death and he could find a place of safety, a home, and a true love. Cliff was Mac's best friend and understood him more than anyone else, yet as Cliff stood there he could not have known the measure of the man and the coldness of the killer known as Murder Incorporated. Cliff could not have known what was coming or the results.

"Well Cliff, I haven't seen anyone at all, I think we have time, let's go down to the Ranch and I will fix us up some Rib eyes for dinner." Mac looked at Cliff smiling

"Sounds good" Cliff answered, and then both followed the narrow trail that wound down the side of the mountain outcropping from where they were at. After some time, they came into the Ranch area and looked around, again no one was seen. Looking at the Ranch house, Mac could see that the door was still intact and locked, the windows all shut tight. "We're still secure Cliff, but let me go first to make sure."

"Wait Mac, let me send Sun and Ray, they will let us know if anything is up"; with that Cliff nodded to Sun and Ray who were looking at him with searching eyes. They seemed to understand Cliff. Cliff grabbed them both, petting them softly and then pointed to the Ranch house and outbuildings, "Sun and Ray, Intruder"!

In a shot, both dogs ran to the house, they were on a mission and looked all around for the intruder, the one-word command that upon a gesture of a hand with it told the two where to go and look for anyone there. In about five minutes the dogs came back and Cliff gave them each a treat for their work. Cliff looked at Mac and said, "Okay Mac, it is safe"

Mac went forward as Cliff backed up a little out of sight, but had enough view to aim his rifle. He followed Mac's every move and as Mac walked; Cliff glassed around the Ranch. Nothing in sight and now Mac went inside. After a few moments, he motioned to Cliff and soon they were in the Ranch house.

In an instant both Sun and Ray perked up and started barking, going toward the road by the corner. Both Mac and Cliff saw the dogs and Mac spoke quickly as they heard a car coming. "Quick Cliff, go out the back door and around the edge to the barn with your rifle you will have a good view of the driveway.

In the next moment Cliff spoke with a clear command "Sun and Ray Here and he pointed at his side", immediately both dogs stopped and turned about as on a dime and in a second were at Cliff's side. The three went through the house and took their positions.

Meanwhile Mac was at the side of the house and waiting. He saw Cliff and the two dogs in place at the edge of the barn looking out at the driveway.

Soon a Maroon SUV drove up and Mac strained to see who it was. It was clearly not the Colonel's men, probably just fishermen looking for a spot to access the creek nearby on his Ranch property. But all this land was private and was closed to all fishing and hunting to outsiders. The driveway was private and you could see that the no trespassing signs were everywhere, yet here they were. Mac came out with his rifle in full view. He could see two characters in the back, they were not the Colonel's men, but even at this distance Mac could see they were armed and also taken aback by seeing the rifle in Mac's hand. In the front seat were two cowpokes, one a younger man who looked familiar and a woman. As Mac came close he saw a smile on the younger of the two in the front. A window rolled down and a voice yelled out "Mac"!

Mac knew that voice immediately, and said "Tiger" as he smiled, and then he walked toward the door as Tiger prepared to get out. Cliff saw these were friendlies so he said "Okay" to both dogs, to which they leaped up and followed Cliff as he came out from around the corner of the barn. Cliff lowered his rifle and saw that Mac had seen Tiger in the SUV.

Gin, Tiger, Bruce, and Paul got out of the SUV. Mac took Tiger and gave him a big hug, smiling; saying "Man I am glad you are alive, you certainly worried your old uncle".

"Sorry Mac for the trouble and causing you to worry and all, but I will explain later." Tiger stopped short. "It is sure great to see you both", said Tiger sounding relieved to be there, as he looked at Mac and Cliff standing there, and then he smiled as he saw Cliff's dogs saying; "Here are Sun and Ray, I love your dogs! When they have puppies again I want one." Tiger squatted down as both dogs recognized him, with affection, the three had a reunion right there.

 "Tiger, glad to see you made it here; we were really worried about you" said Cliff relieved and looking around he started to introduce himself and shake hands with Gin, Bruce, and Paul.

Mac looked at the three, and then Tiger introduced his friends. When all the greetings were over; they all headed to the porch. As they all got comfortable and the extended hugging between Mac and Tiger were over; they sat on the chairs lining the porch. Cliff got some pop and beer that had been in Mac's fridge and handed them out, a beer for the three men and a pop for Gin and Tiger. By now the sun was over the hill behind them and the pines cast a shadow towards the

Ranch. The fire had been stoked earlier and now Cliff put on more logs. The fire would heat the place up; company had arrived and all were happy that they could be together. But on this night, as the joy of the reunion went on and the steaks were being prepared on the Ranch open pit fireplace, as they laughed and told of what happened; Mac still felt uneasy.

Now he had others to get out alive, he knew the Colonels men were close and soon the real fireworks would begin. Mac settled in his chair and watched Cliff bring up the steaks and plate them with a bake potato and baked beans. As he ate Mac looked around, everyone was happy and smiling. Tiger looked at his Uncle and saw the worry on his face; he also knew trouble was not far away!

Mac looked at Tiger and was happy he was with him and safe; but the project and its leaders will stop at nothing to quell resistance, plug holes in security, and do anything it takes to bring in their vision of a world that would project a black light into the hearts of men. A light that brings with it delusion and deception and right now, only Mac really knew the full truth of the Colonel and the secret project he heads up for those in high places. After all, it was Mac who helped to start it up!

As the night settled in and the reunion went on, the forces of evil gathered to battle with the forces of good. But in this war, the goal was simple for those who wanted to Steel the Darkness. They would wage war and they would win, nothing would stop them. Of this they were certain.

Chapter Four: Agenda

There are many devices in a man's heart; nevertheless the counsel of the LORD, that shall stand Proverbs 19:21

It was level thirteen, of all the many level's, where no one wanted to go. If you went there as an enemy combatant, you never came back. But even level 13 or 'purgatory' as it was jokingly called had an attraction to those who did the bidding of people over them in the project. People who worked this level never saw the light of day, let alone public entertainment like movies, plays, or going out to eat. The place was self-contained with full rooms better than the finest hotel would have. It was also the only level with its own movies, game room, and a restaurant with every cuisine known to man. All guards had a badge with the number 666 on it. 666 was simply the number of a man, and in this domain on the thirteenth level there was a difference between men, demons, and fallen angels. It was so that all humans, men and women alike had the badge with this number.

This level was the main arena for two top level programs which operated. Like all black projects, these were funneled out of earlier programs and projects of the government. The first began with what some called Majic by insiders or Majestic 12 or MJ-12 to the conspiracy theorists. It was a cover project which was intended to be a ploy for those who thought more on the alien and UFO agenda than they should. The first to really call it out was William Cooper who had uncovered a lot about the secret projects. But even with Cooper's death and the uncovering of the MJ-12 documents among others, these all provided for the real plan to go ahead. The truth being is by the time you actually think you have gotten one up on the secrets of this government; it is then that you really don't know anything at all. They provided you something to find. That is the way they work. The government in D.C., even the President, congress, and the rich and powerful have no clue as to the real agenda. On level 13, it is that agenda which runs 25 hours a day, seven days a week. Yes, their clock is 25 hours, by adding one extra hour; they are sure to use up all the hours in a day. They placed central human lighting technology that produced colors in all spectrums. In this way, it created emotional and physical wellbeing. In one corner of the bunker on level thirteen is a huge granite wall of rock. It is into this wall to which bars are drilled that makes the entry way to the lock up secure. The lock up was up a level, so a metal staircase led up to the entry way of the lock up. The bars are titanium and with electronic locks and guards, if you are put in there, then death is a better option. In one corner of the lockups are smaller cages, where the human cloning, DNA experiments have created creatures that don't even have names. Those who experiment here are top scientists, Physicists, and doctors who have more in common with Hitler's Mengele than with any American. They work to bring about the fundamental changes in DNA and cloning. Today many have seen some of their more successful experiments become top level. That is, they use it for their own agenda. For instance, when people see Bigfoot or any of his related kin; it is really a creature created here and then released into society above. The animal itself was the result of a DNA experiment that created a creature humanlike but also part ape. He would be smarter, more powerful than apes, but also not have all the reasoning faculties of humans. They have placed these in China, the upper northwest, the Rockies, and the swamps of the south. In all this, humans are needed so in the provision of that need, their Alien friends come in handy. All extra human traces not needed are destroyed in acid baths which make up a portion of the area in the main labs. No traces left, except for the semi human odd-looking creatures looking out from the cages deep within level thirteen in the lock up area. Everything here is strictly business, nothing personal, no compassion and the soldiers there are hardened.

Off to one side, to the far left of the Elevator there is a pyramid with one eye on a gold plaque. To the right of it is a set of doors, made of very heavy mahogany with silver handles. These two doors make into one double door with an upside-down cross on both doors engraved in the wood. To the right of the double doors is a shoulder high plaque with a book on a stand attached to it. The words Lucifer can be seen engraved in the plaque. It is the place where everyone who entered through the double doors had to swear. They would look at the plaque, read the words out loud while placing both their hands on the book. The book is the dark book of curses, which if you failed on your oath to Lucifer; you would die by these curses. The only ones who entered through these doors were a secretive group of people who visited. They came around every Solstice and only the Colonel along with the General from the main office visited with them. They would all go into those chambers and come out several hours later.

Some rumors had it that it led to hell itself and Lucifer's throne. But no one knew, if they did; they would never divulge what was behind those doors. A power came over them and when they came out; you could see the change in them and if you looked closely; their eyes revealed it all. The eye is the window to the soul. In these eyes, no soul could be seen; only darkness. Their eyes would stay that way for several hours and then return to normal.

In the far end from the elevator, was a secure room that had a laser lock and two guards, and then another door flanked by two more guards. This was the entryway into the C.A.C.F., or the Central Alien Command Force. In this area were many different types of entities. Even the ones in contact with these creatures did not really know where they came from. All they could do was believe what they were told. Officials though, know that among the entities here are inter dimensional space travelers, others are beings that live here on earth; some in the cities under the seas and others beneath the earth. Here you could find the small grey's who look alike. You also had the very tall very humanoid looking Pleiadeans, which were a little paler than a normal human. But with little makeup could pass for human. Then there were the Nordic aliens, the Lizard looking ones, and many others. That was one portion of the area humans could not go into. It was there that if you went in, the mere contact with these aliens would kill you. Years ago, when these were first discovered, officials sent in their best team to confront the visitors. They were dead in moments by some strange disease. Now only trained scientists in a full decontamination suits can go in and work with them.

In the center of this was the main desk. At the desk the Colonel was standing talking with Eloneh and Londo. These two Pleiadeans were the two who walked among the humans. In fact, only their kind could do so without much trouble. The Pleiadeans are an ancient race of humans living in the Pleiades star system of 1,400 stars. They are very technologically advanced as is their ability to communicate with others without speaking out loud. They are not violent and abhor the alien races that are violent and bloody. They also know of the Nephilim and have encountered them. But the Pleiadeans will defend themselves and are quite adept at doing so. They think of humans as their children and constantly tell everyone that they created man. They have come back to help man over the next stage

of their evolution. It is their technology that has helped America in

her tech war.

"You know how important it is to keep the crafts moving in and out

of areas, then! We want people to see the crafts and even at times see

the occupants. But you are not to directly contact any of them unless

we tell you. Of course, we do continue to want you to pick up

specimens and bring them here for further use. We also want young

children to implant and track. It is important for the project that we

keep people's minds on other things while we get ready for the next

move." The Colonel finished and then looked at Eloneh and Londo.

Londo stood erect and beside him Eloneh, the female of the two.

Although the Pleiadeans communicated among themselves and at

times with humans telepathically, when with the Colonel it was an

audible voice the Colonel heard and when they spoke perfect English

was heard. The Pleiadeans had the ability to immediately know all

known human languages, but the use of English was the preferred

one. As far as being Pleiadeans, they were perfect humanoid

specimens, looking almost exactly human, except their eyes being blue, had no pupils. Their hair was a perfect golden blonde, so much

so it looked like it was dyed.

"Yes Colonel, we understand and we have just finished the Israel

quadrant and even those we have contacted there believe our people

are Gods. We are ready for the Phoenix advancement, and are

preparing for the larger Moscow appearance to take place very

soon." Londo finished and smiled, and then he looked at Eloneh.

"Colonel, when can we become more personally associated with the

humans we contact? How can we truly help them to prepare for their

next step in evolution if we don't help them?" Eloneh questioned

"I quite understand Eloneh, I will get in touch with C.A.C.F. main

force directives and find out. I am sure it will be okay to proceed in

the not too distant future!" The Colonel finished, and then said, "Is

there anything else you want to report?"

"No Colonel" answered Londo as he and Eloneh prepared to leave.

 "Well, then I must be going", with that the Colonel headed to the

Elevator to go back to his main floor.

As the Colonel opened the elevator and looked out, he saw the lock

up area. He could hear the various creatures all crying out, and from

time to time terrible screams echoed in the place. He was glad to be leaving. Even as hardened and dark as the Colonel was, this place gave him the creeps. He is dealing with creatures, yes aliens that think differently than humans do. They will seem to work with you, but you must watch what they say. In dealing with them you really do not know if they are telling you the truth. In addition, the real agenda as to why they are working with us is also not known. One thing is for sure, the Colonel did not trust anyone, especially these Aliens. But the Colonel would use them to serve the purpose of their Global Agenda. They had killed some of them before; it could be done again if they got out of hand. The door closed and soon the Colonel was in his office looking out at the desert, "good this is better, I know this view" thinking to himself as he shivered a little "from nerves he thought", and then turned to finish his report to the General.

"Sir we found them" he stopped, listened, and then said, "About 3 clicks northwest". He stopped again, pausing briefly then spoke "Yes sir, if we can we will bring Mac in alive; but I thought it was a kill order. The soldier then grimaced as a loud indistinguishable sound could be heard." The soldier hung up the secure Sat phone. He looked at the men, all dressed in black fatigues, black hats, boots, and with some cameo makeup on. All eyes looked at their leader who spoke. They had come in unmarked SUV's specially equipped with surveillance equipment, computers, and non-traceable license plates.

"Some plans have changed; we are to take Mac alive, seems some of the higher ups want this guy alive as they have plans for him." The platoon leader stopped, and then looked over his men. They were well prepared for anything. They were the black ops secret military squads, comprised of former secret snipers, CIA hit men, and Special Forces. With the latest in technology, bullet proof vests, night vision equipment, radar, drones, and other kill tools at their disposal not to many people got away from them. They had a 91% success acquisition rate, but then they mostly went against just one or two targets at a time. Mac was different, his techniques were used in training exercises and it was Mac who literally wrote the book on killing. He has the record for the most successful target acquisition kills of any sniper. He can find, acquire, and kill his targets 96% of the time. The other 4% is due to weather or other circumstances beyond his control but in a pure target shooting practice with perfect conditions he hit his targets dead on all of the time.

Mac looked out at the early morning mist rising off the natural spring, he turned and got a cup of coffee and went outside to the porch. The dogs were resting on the porch, if they were not alarmed, then no one was near enough to do any harm. Cliff was in the barn working on something and the rest were just rising. A skillet of potatoes, onions, jalapeno's, were covered after being fried. Another pan had some scrambled eggs, while fried bacon lay neatly on a paper towel sitting on a plate. Everything looked peaceful, but on the horizon a very dark menacing cloud could be seen.

As Mac watched the horizon, his senses were on alert. He adjusted his 457 in his side holster and checked his pockets for extra rounds. His survival knife was also strapped to his leg, while he had another very sharp knife, a throwing knife inserted in his belt. He had on his fatigues and in his pockets, back up materials like a choker chain with spikes in it to kill with, compass, phone, and keys. Cliff came out of the barn and had his rifle. He walked across to the main house and stopped where Mac stood on the porch sipping coffee. He looked at Mac and then spoke:

"I grabbed my armor piercing shells yesterday and in checking my rifle I also found more rounds than I thought I had. If someone comes at us and has bullet proof vests, these little babies will go clean through" Cliff finished and smiled as he held an armor piercing round.

"Well if you do that be sure you aim directly for a vital, because if you hit the wrong area the bullet will simply pass through the vest and the body doing little damage. He would be well enough to kill you after you shot him, so shoot for the vitals, okay?" Mac finished

"Yes, I will. But Mac, I am going to get some breakfast and then go find a place to watch from. If they do come I want to be ready to hit first."

"Well if you do go and find a vantage point, be sure you're well-hidden because these guys are professionals and know how to spot amateurs who think they are hidden. Take some cameo and makeup with you, cut limbs and bushes; surround yourself with nature and don't let the sun reflect your glasses or scope. Don't give your position away. Fire once, then move, fire again, then move; etc. Don't fire twice from the same place if you can." Mac stopped, and then added "be careful"!

"Really Mac, I am not new to this" Answered Cliff harshly looking squarely at Mac

"I know it is just that I don't want you hit my friend. I'm sorry, over protective, just be careful and yes I know how you are in a firefight and I would not want anyone else on my side my friend." With that Mac stopped and patted him on the back.

Cliff smiled at Mac and turned to go inside.

At breakfast all the group sat around the ranch house some in the kitchen others by the fire and they ate quietly. Gin sat by the fire stirring her potato's and eggs together and looked at Mac and Cliff who were discussing something.

She put down her plate and moved her hands against the fireplace and warmed them. She was "chilly and this fire feels good" she thought. Gin sat watching Tiger finishing up his breakfast and took a swig of fresh spring water. He put the glass down and it fell over. Then a rumble was followed by another rumble. The light fixtures began to move violently, the kitchen cupboards opened and dishes began falling out onto the floor. The Rumbling continued as Mac and Cliff scrambled into the living room near the rest of the group. "Earthquake" yelled Mac questioning what he was experiencing; then adding "we don't get earthquakes like this!"

Cliff moved to a close wall and supported himself "this is not normal guys" he muttered

The quake continued for what seemed like an eternity, then stopped abruptly. Then all of some sudden hard thumps hit the roof of the Ranch house.

"Hail, in summer" screamed Mac, "Now I know what's going on"!

The Hail beat down for several moments then stopped and it quieted down.

Cliff looked at Mac puzzled, then rain started beating down, like a river it came in sheets.

"Something's up Mac" yelled Gin

"Mac, what is going on" asked Tiger looking at his uncle

"I am not sure, but I know who is behind it, get your guns; Cliff find your spot, get the dogs ready" Mac grabbed his auto and went with a handful of clips to the side as he grabbed his glasses and looked out.

"Nothing yet" he said; "come on let's go"

As Mac went outside he moved quickly to the barn, then to the pines, where he took up a spot. Cliff had run ahead and was heading to a vantage point up above the ranch. By now Mac was wet and the rain was coming down very hard.

Both Bruce and Paul grabbed their guns and took up positions in the cabin with Tiger and Gin.

It stopped as quickly as it started. Like a sign or something; the weather was now clearing. But Mac new that this triggered something and he noticed something in the distance and as Mac breathed deep, he saw movement across the pasture, there they are. He looked up at Cliff and motioned to him the direction. He could see Cliff acknowledging it.

Then off to the left he saw two soldiers closing in on the house and bullets rang out and one of the men fell. The other scrambled to the side of the barn. Mac had leveled his sniper rifle and was carefully choosing targets. He had sighted it in the other day and the system felt good. Mac zeroed in on a black clothed figure moving from one tree to another. Mac squeezed the trigger in a smooth motion and the figure fell. He quickly took a bead on someone else and hit him directly in the head; down he went like a sack of rocks. In rapid succession, Mac had taken out three of the Colonels men.

Then Mac moved a bit and a bullet rang out hitting just above his head, coming from the timber across from him. He took careful aim and with the scope looked for signs of movement, but saw nothing.

Then another bullet rang out and a light reflected off the Sun that had just came out. Now Mac could clearly see, "a sniper", thought Mac; well indeed this is your last job. But as Mac rolled over to the tree to get a shot at the sniper another shot rang out and hit right by him. He then moved to a large boulder that was close to him. The sniper could not see him. He crossed back into the woods and went to the right. He looked carefully and suddenly to the left he noticed a figure of a man out of the corner of his eye. Instinct took over as he moved quickly to one side and took the soldier down. The man had his rifle knocked down and was in a struggle for his life, but Mac's years of training were instinct and he quickly got a lock on his head and gave a quick twist breaking his neck. The body went limp and Mac saw a young man of about 23. He was sad, Mac hated this; but they came after him. Mac heard a howl and looked up, Cliff could be seen struggling with someone and his two dogs had someone pinned. Running fast out of sight, he saw someone to the left of the boulder he had just came from and a piercing pain hit him in the arm. He went down and suddenly the man was on him. Mac fought for all he was worth. With the injury, the pain was nothing; it was bleeding and made everything slippery. He got ahold of the man and heard a curse, and then Mac slid his knife out of his belt and stabbed him in the heart. The man lay down limply and immediately Mac saw it was one of the very ones he had trained so many years ago. He could not remember the name, but knew the face as one who knew the techniques Mac taught. Mac grabbed his rifle as he moved to the edge of a large tree and scoped the area for the sniper. Then, He saw the sniper, but barely; as he had moved and was covered in cameo and leaves. But Mac knew the ropes that snipers used. He took aim and adjusted the scope. He lined it up and gently squeezed the trigger. The gun dropped in the distance and through the scope Mac saw him roll to the side and not move. His arm was not bleeding as much now. Mac grabbed his arm and quickly put some blood clot powder on it and wrapped it up. It throbbed but also looked like the bullet had passed through a muscle and out the back. He reached the area where Cliff was and saw two dead bodies. Cliff was nursing a knife wound on his thigh.

"You okay?" Mac asked

"Yes, just a scratch; but the dogs had a time" Cliff answered

The two shepherds, Sun and Ray came to Mac; they were bloodied and bruised but not too bad for the experience. Two more shots rang out and both Cliff and Mac looked out and now Paul was giving a

pro wrestler lesson to some soldier as Bruce checked the body of

another man. Mac scoped the area and saw some more men

approaching.

We have more at 2 o clock, with that Mac looked at Cliff; I will take

the ones on the right you got the left; start to shoot in 3-2-1 Now and

the bullets rang out. Mac hit one of the men and then moved quickly

to reach the others. Cliff had put in his armor piercing shells and he

hit one of them right away in the chest, and soon Cliff had hit the

other one who tried to take cover. Bruce had seen them and picked

them up, shooting one in stomach and the other one started running

off to the left. Mac was nowhere to be seen; then he appeared at the

side of the barn. Both Gin and Tiger saw him and two men were

heading right into him. As they watched, they yelled to Mac to warn

him, but he did not hear them. Cliff was now glassing all around and

could only see the one black SUV head off out of the area.

Mac could hear them coming and in a moment, he was a mad man,

he had his razor sharp knife in his left hand and as he came out he

sliced the throat of the nearest soldiers and as he did his other hand

instinctively fired the pistol into the mid-section of the other soldier.

Mac looked around and for now, there was no one around him. The two lay on the ground bleeding profusely, they had been taken out. Mac and Cliff joined up and headed to the house. They found two bodies inside the Ranch house where Tiger had shot them both as they came in. Bruce was nursing Paul who was down. Mac could see Bruce also had a small wound and asked if all was okay.

"I'm fine and considering what just happened, I would say this is a good day; we lived through it!" Bruce looked at his wound and pulled a piece of cloth around it. He would take care of it later, he then grabbed Paul and put his arm around him and helped him to the house.

Mac and Cliff along with Sun and Ray stood on the porch glassing the area. In all a group of Black SUV's; with men had come upon them. Two of the Black vehicles were still there; and a third had made a getaway and in the process the whereabouts of Mac's hideout had been compromised.

Gin, Tiger, Bruce, and Paul were in the main living room, finishing bandaging wounds and cleaning up. Logs were on the fire as everyone began to calm down and realize they had made it through one of the Colonels hit squads.

Cliff sat on a chair and leaned it against the Ranch wall as he began looking out from the porch to the surrounding area. He looked at Mac as he dialed a number. He knew who he was calling. This was the other side of Mac that only he knew.

"Mac here, yes they hit as expected" Mac looked at Cliff while listening to some unknown voice on the other end; "Yes we have been compromised and we need a cleaner ASAP." Waiting again, Mac stood and looked around the room as he said, "No sir we are all fine, yes I will tell them, we are proceeding on as planned" with that Mac hung up.

As Mac talked on the phone he was seen by both Tiger and Gin as they came through the doorway and onto the porch. They both looked at each other surprised and then yelled at Mac.

"Did I hear you say that you expected this?" Roared Tiger and Gin together, as Paul and Bruce who were on the porch looked at him in agreement, saying "Okay Mac what is really going on here"!

Mac looked at them "There is nothing secretive going on here, that is; from you guys! Did you really think that these guys would just stop coming because you came to this Ranch?" Mac stopped and looked directly at them!

"Well No" cried Tiger as Gin nodded in agreement. But who were you talking to?

"There are people who I call on from time to time. Suffice it to say, we are not in this alone and they are glad you are all fine" Mac stopped, and then added "We must leave this area fast, there will be people coming to clean up the place, trust me; no law officer will be able to enter or ask questions, these guys coming are specialists but also they are backed by the highest law credentials in our Government". With that the questions stopped and everyone took a breather.

Gin looked up and said, "I must get back to the Remnant group, the meeting is coming fast." Tiger looked at Mac and said "I have to go as well Mac".

"I know you do Tiger, I was planning on coming with you, I wanted to thank this Reverend friend of yours, who rescued my nephew!" Mac stopped and looked at Cliff, he opened his eyes and said, "Well I might as well go along; I will leave the dogs in town with some friends."

The sun was setting and the place was again beginning to seem like a nice mountain get away. But as they sat there they knew the Colonel would re-group.

In all, they had been very lucky thought Mac as he walked. He went out by the barn and took in a deep breath of fresh air. It does smell good in this high country. As he looked around he noticed in the far corner of the pasture, up on a hill over-looking it was a dark figure bathed in shadows from the evening sun. Mac looked at it, but did not make it out. It was a figure, but could not tell much. Soon the figure disappeared.

Looking down, the figure clothed in shadows saw Mac and was glad everyone was now safe. He had been there the whole time. Behind him was another person. He was totally out of view, he looked at the figure before him asked "Prophet when are you going to reveal yourself to them?"

"Soon, very soon; it is not the Lords timing yet; we will do our work behind the scenes for the glory of the Lord"

The Prophet turned around and said "Benjamin, we must be going"! With that the Prophet, nicknamed the Sage brush Prophet got in the car. Benjamin was behind the wheel and did the driving. The

Prophet sat back and closed his eyes saying, "let me know when we get close to home, I have some work to do tonight."

As they drove back into the brush and sage from whence he came, he did so as a shadow and moved out of reach like lightning. Yet most of what people said about him was exaggeration. He was merely a man, but also a real honest to God Prophet. But do not underestimate who he was; for miracles and signs confirmed his work. He was called of God and anointed, and then there was the pouring of oil on his head by the angel who worked with him. He was a last day Prophet. The Tanakh says to "fear God and the Prophets", for fear is the beginning of wisdom. You did not mess with the Prophet.

The Colonel was fuming and no one could console him. He had sent his best men after Mac and all were now dead or missing. He knew if any were alive, they would not see the light of day. All of it was covert. The one left alive was now in debriefing on level thirteen. He would never see the surface again. But one thing he knew now, he was not just facing Mac, there were others with him and they like Mac knew how to kill.

"General, all are dead except for one and we are debriefing him" the Colonel stopped as he heard the General start speaking:

"Colonel you know what to do with the one survivor see to it, as for this Mac is it true you told them to take him alive?"

"Yes General, I know we can turn him, just give him to me and my boys on level 13; he will come on board", The Colonel chuckled

"No Colonel, from now on take no chances with this Mac or those with him. Kill on sight as I don't want any more of our men killed over this. Make sure you don't mess up again Colonel. You have really gotten into the deep pool of the abyss Colonel with this. We want it quiet, not advertised. We don't need a civil war between you and Mac. You are risking the project if you expose what we do to the public eye. Do you understand me Colonel?" The General stopped, then added; "and be sure Colonel everyone is expendable."

"Don't worry General; I will take care of this! No worries here!"

"That's right Colonel I don't need any worries about this." The Generals voice was visibly raised and shaking

"Yes sir", the Colonel was now going to get Mac; he had cost him valuable trust with the organization. He could not afford to mess this up. In spite of the Generals warning, the Colonel would do it his way! Besides, if the General causes more trouble, then he would simply take out the General. The Colonel had done this before. He was his own boss and only chose to acknowledge those supposedly over him. Yes, he would proceed his way and if his boss causes trouble, well he would take him out! For the Colonel, this was personal and indeed it had become a war; a damn big war and he would make sure Mac was dead and all those with him. He immediately was on the phone "get me three more SUV's and fill them with our hit teams. I also want a resource van with all the standard equipment and forward all my calls to my mobile. Also prepare me a drone and yes I want it armed. Feed into the status instructions the current descriptions of Mac and everyone associated with him. I want kill orders on sight for them all. I will be out of the office until some business is taken care of".

The Colonel got his stuff packed and readied to go. He would lead the hit teams on Mac. He would kill Mac and come back here and let the cleaner's tidy things up. In the whole scheme of the Colonel's mind he would also find the main Remnant group that they knew was in the area near Mac. He would take them out and destroy their headquarters. What the General didn't know couldn't hurt him! In spite of warnings from his superiors the Colonel always went ahead on his own. He risked his own life and trust within the agency itself by going on his own. He had always done things this way and always pulled it off and this time it would be no different. Even if he had to call in a drone strike, he would 'kill them all and let their God sort it all out'! The Colonel laughed out loud as he thought of his success. He had never lost a hit, he was the man! This time the Colonel was coming and with him was death. But secretly the Colonel admired Mac and his skill set. He wanted Mac, but wanted him at his side. But the Colonel knew how dangerous a game this can be. If he was smart, he would kill Mac and forget it; but something in the Colonel knew how valuable Mac was; if only he could turn him!

In the desert, a light is on in a Ranch house. In one corner is a young man writing in a journal. He was very carefully putting down the words he was told.

"Benjamin did you get that?" asked the Prophet

"Yes I did" answered Benjamin, the Prophets scribe who carefully recorded all that occurred and any message he was given to record. As Benjamin looked over the writing, he corrected some words, and looked at the Prophet who now was sipping a hot tea with honey. The Prophet looked at him and motioned with his head nodding that they were about to begin again. With that, the Prophet spoke and Benjamin wrote the words down.

"In the chaos of the struggle between light and darkness, there were many trapped in-between. Everyone had friends, relatives, wives, husbands, lovers, and lived in America. The trouble was the separation of America by two powerful viewpoints; howbeit secret powers of how the nation should proceed. At one end were the constitutionalists, who many times were conservative Christians; but also in their midst were liberals, warriors, agnostics, atheists, and others. The Remnant had grown from a small few of what some called 'motley constitutionalists' to a vast unseen army. It had become large, mainly because the White House along with congress departed from the many rights found in the constitution. But there also existed for many decades a group that made use of the new more liberal socialism that had gained steam. Even in Political America people divided the battle to one of liberal verses conservative; while others defined the split as one between constitutionalists and states' rights which was opposed by a stricter

Federalism. The battle was not so easy to define because the real battle is one which many Americans did not see. By the time they do see it; it will be too late to stop the revolution that will be upon them. This would be the rift to begin the great civil war which would occur on the land. This war would be greater in scope than the first civil war and this time America would not end its wars united, but divided. Yes America would divide after the great cataclysm and be no more. The forces are locked in battle as they now position themselves for the greater struggle which will begin soon.

The two opposing forces flowed secretly but powerfully from beneath the Pentagon. They were the ones from which the battle had been going on for years. This flowed from certain rich and powerful supporters through to the separate sources to which these people were joined with. One went beyond a mere one world government, to one that had no defining of nations, no borders of individual peoples. It was one where there was a one world leader and those who followed him, and they ruled over the nations. Then there were the ones who knew that such an arrangement had been revealed in many sacred writings and it was these people who stood against the forces of such change. On this side were many people, many faiths, and many beliefs. They simply wanted freedom and independent

nations as it had always been. It was into this arena that the one side,

was able to tap into the forces of evil and the ability to do as Hitler

had done. Hitler had managed to get the technology and help from

Alien forces. He was bringing in the Holy Roman German Empire.

But he failed and the ones who followed him had brought with them

the ability to communicate with otherworldly entities in order to use

for their goals. This group had been in America already since the

early beginnings; they were people who did not like the path

America had taken. It was an ongoing battle and in the midst of all

this; people would die. Someone would win, others would lose! It

was a battle of light and darkness. But the battles were covert and

society knew nothing about it. Yet the struggle would literally

destroy the nation, this was the goal. To reduce nationalist

individuality and people's right and bring in the rule of one person.

That one will be the dark one who will rise spoken of in Revelation

chapter 13."

"It was into the midst of this that God had sent his Prophet. It

was a call since childhood and he was a Jew, a Levitical Priest, and

one that Angels did appear to. He was instructed by the Word of

God, the Angels who God sent, and through open visions. His work at this point was a direct message to America of Judgment and to collect the Remnant. This was not the Remnant of people in America, but of the Remnant of God, true born-again believers who according to Revelation 'kept the commandments of God and the faith and testimony of Jesus'. He worked to bring in those who truly were the Remnant. These were according to Revelation chapter 12 and verse 11 believers 'who overcame by the blood of the Lamb, the word of their testimony, and loved not their lives unto death.' It would be these, as it says in Revelation Chapter twelve and verse 17 that the dragon would war against, those who 'are the remnant of her seed, which keep the commandments of God, and have the testimony of Jesus Christ.' Furthermore, it is the 'patience of these saints', which during this end of days war would be a factor of who they were but also there was another point that they would 'keep the commandments of God, and the faith of Jesus' according to Revelation chapter fourteen and verse 12. Here during the end of days stood a true Prophet that worked in the supernatural, with signs and wonders battling darkness. It was this battle and the bringing in of the Remnant that was the work''.

The Prophet finished and sat down. He had been walking to and fro speaking these words for the record. Benjamin was very astute in what he did for the Prophet. No one worked as close to him as he did. But while he was the Prophet's scribe, there were others who helped to protect, keep, and care for the Prophet and the Ranch on which they all lived. They all had been with him for many years and had seen many miracles. So miraculous in fact that many Christians refused to believe them. But the calling and building of the Remnant was being done by the Lord, and daily people were added to the group. They came from all over, while some who came to know him; simply stayed where they were and worked with the Prophet in the end of days Remnant. Yet this group was nonpolitical, non-denomination, and truly a prophetic end of day's ministry. These believers followed the end of day's marching orders in Revelation, keeping the commandments of God and the faith and testimony of Jesus Christ [Yeshua Ha Massiach].

As the Prophet finished, he felt a little tired. It had been a long day. He sat in his chair and relaxed. The Hot tea had warmed him and he felt comfy. In his spirit he knew that the battle would be heating up. The enemy in these last days would be responsible for many deaths, yet as he sat there, sleep came to him. Benjamin looked over and saw the Prophet sleeping, he had some things to finish in the journal; and then he too would head to the bunkhouse to rest.

As the Prophet and his people slept, in the Spirit realm you could see the dark powers moving across the land. Green clouds of mist seem to cover the landscape and in it was filth. In the distance from all major directions false prophetic spirits rose up to prophesy. These entities were dressed in brown robes, and looked like a Priest. But if you saw their faces, you would see sheer blackness. Out of these entities spewed filth and false prophecies. On the Prophets Ranch on every corner were posted huge guardian angels with very large flaming swords. They were full of light and nothing of the darkness crossed over. This was the realm of the Prophet and tonight, the "Angels of the Lord were encamped round about" the Prophet and his people, just like they had done every night and every day. Benjamin finished and then took a throw blanket and put it over the Prophet. He turned off the lights and went outside. The night sky was exhilarating and he could smell the fresh air mixed with pine. Somewhere a wooden fireplace or campfire was going, he smelled the wood burning. As he walked, he prayed and thanked the Lord for the day. It was a good day and tomorrow was another day in the end of days. He had a front row seat and for that he was glad. A night owl was hooting in the distance and crickets sang a night song. Good night Lord, he said and soon was in bed sleeping.

Chapter Five: Underfoot

Lest Satan should get an advantage of us: for we are not ignorant of his devices. 2 Corinthians 2:11

A little over four hours from D.C. the little town sat nestled among other eastern seaboard towns. But this was not just an ordinary town; it had historical and cultural value. Aside from that, the town was the home of many hedge funds and financial services companies. Two men sat at a table talking quietly and casually and to the untrained observer you would never have known who they were. If money is power, then these two lacked nothing in that regard. But their connections to nefarious black projects were never known in this small town of about sixty thousand. Had the residents known of the plots going on in their midst, they would have hung them up. These were just two of the secret voices that had major influence in Project Black Light. They monitor all activity, news, and other reports and what they heard coming out of the Midwest was not good. It was too much attention and the cost could be too high.

The two sat there as they sipped their Asparagus Soup with Lobster and scallops. They were also drinking from a bottle of the finest French vintage wine.

"Is it not too risky to have such a gad about killing everything in sight" spoke one to the other as he eyed the room around them

"Yes, it most assuredly is and we are too close to have anyone mess this up" the other answered and added "it is all secretive; it is supposed to be done efficiently, so that the public has no idea."

"Who is in charge there?" the other asked as he took a piece of lobster and mouthed the delicacy

"The General as they call him is the chief of Alpha section, but the real trouble is the Colonel. He is really someone straight out of the cold war spy movies. He is evil, secretive, bloody, and very good at killing and getting things done. But now, he has become sloppy" was the reply

"We do not worry about some opposition, we must let them be. The Presidency is ours and since our people had been able to get the Homeland Security Act Passed, then everything was set for the takeover. This meant that when we trigger the red flag event here in America, then this law will be the ladder for absolute control of this country. No one can do a thing about it and the real cause will be terrorism and not some nut case in the Midwest. The threat will be someone from the outside who has managed to slip in. Further the extreme regimes like Iran and North Korea with their threats against the US only makes it a more viable plot. You see people will believe that these people had sent infiltrators to damage our country. To prove to us we are vulnerable, to get us to bend a little in our policies. These are all valid reasons why they would indeed send a terrorist into this country. We will use this to our advantage."

The other man nodded in agreement and said "Even Israel and her actions against Iran would prove to our benefit, which we could use. What these Jihadists don't figure on is that their fighting and terrorism helps us bring in our New World Order. By their actions we can lock down a nation and no one would be the wiser for it. The Terrorists would be to blame, not us!" He stopped and took a drink and spoke again "We must watch the situation carefully and if it gets out of hand, then you know what to do!"

"Yes, sir will do, we will let you know of developments, besides when it goes down we have the military, there will be the camps, and total martial law will be initiated. Our legal teams are preparing documents for the right time and will present these. The United States had internment camps before and the legal teams believe with the Justices on the court now, that they will agree to internment camps again. Because we are at War, any opposition will be crushed." He stopped and looked at his superior who added; "We also have the lists and before it goes down, we will be in place to pick up tens of thousands of people who will be on the kill list while others on the re-education lists."

The other listened intently as he continued his delicious meal. He thought to himself, 'here he was in the most expensive French restaurant on the eastern seaboard with the finest cuisine taking care of issues that will fundamentally change America and not one soul in this restaurant is any the wiser for it'. He mused over this and chuckled to himself, which went unnoticed by the other patrons sitting across from them. Outside were two limo's and several black SUV's and around them a dozen or more men, dressed to kill; wearing attire that would go well at the Oscars. They were pleasant to each other and those who passed. They would also kill you in a second if you were a threat to them. Not all things are as they seem, not in America. Not anymore, that is! You have to look closely in order to see clearly what is going on and many were simply blind to it all. That is the way these people liked it, enabling them to get away with the things they have been doing.

Alpha Base had sent a resource van with satellite hookup, computers, radar, listening capabilities, and much more ahead of the Colonel. By now the two known as Satan and Lucifer had reported in. They were on the Colonel's black list because of how everything went down. While these two dawdled around, killing some innocent woman, and then left to go search out Mac in Montana; the Colonels men had found Mac. But the Colonel needed these two and their bloody skills and their ability to bring sheer terror into their work would be advantage to getting Mac. Because if the word is true that the girl these two killed was Mac's girl, then he knew mac would vow vengeance. By this the Colonel would let it leak out that the ones who killed her would be at such and such location. He knew Mac would then take the bait and come after them. But before all that they had to move against this base they had found. Their contact within the Remnant group had pinpointed a base outside of Livingston Montana.

Now the van was off the road in some secluded trees and the suspect base was across the roadway some distance back against a hill. Even from this distance they could see everything going on. Between the military version of Google earth and the drone which was going to be showing up soon, nothing would escape them. In addition to the Van, there was a black SUV security detail squad of heavily armed men which sat off to one side. They were here to assess what would be needed to carry out the elimination of the threat target. If they needed to, a drone strike would be called in. From the monitor you could see two people outside what looked like a ranch. There were no signs of anything going on.

Lieutenant Peterson was in charge and he had one other controller who took care of the operation of the equipment. The Lieutenant called the Colonel who answered "Yes, Lieutenant Do you have them on surveillance yet?"

"Yes, Colonel we have them and have been watching the place for a half a day. There is nothing that would suggest that this is a Remnant hideout. There is only a couple here, a man and a woman. No one is coming or going. We have them as the Lazy R Ranch, owners Bob and Tillie Owens. He is a retired military analyst who with his wife bought this ranch ten years ago. It really just looks like any other Ranch out here sir" the Lieutenant stopped.

"That is the idea, to look like any other Ranch. This is what the Remnant does well! Now be sure to keep monitoring. If that is a Remnant Group, I want to know." The Colonel stopped and thought a moment then asked, "How many men do you have there?"

"Sir, me and Williams, plus the other squad outside" he stopped and looked around the van waiting for an answer.

"Can you have your men do a recon of the Ranch after dark? See if you can prove that it is indeed a Remnant hideout. If it is a Remnant group, then report back to me ASAP! I will advise you as to the next move." The Colonel finished and the Lieutenant could hear the urgency in his voice "Yes Sir" the Lieutenant said and disconnected.

The time was 2 am and a group of darkly clad figures make their way to recon the Ranch. These men were all veterans and had fought in Iraq, but they also did black ops missions after that. They had been in the Philippines, Syria, Libya, Ukraine, and other areas for Operation Seclusion. Now they were again in a secretive operation with Project Black Light. As they moved into the Ranch area, their AK's were up to their eyes as they scoped the darkness with the infrared scopes. It was quiet except for the crickets, frogs, and the hoot of an owl. These men moved quietly and at night they were their best. There were no signs of any dogs as the team scanned the perimeter. They made their way to the barn and went inside. A quick look at the area revealed nothing to indicate anything but a typical Ranch Barn. They went out back of the barn, heading to the out buildings. There were two and each house came into view and the teams split up. The first house had no curtains on it and a quick look inside showed it was empty. The other of the two houses had curtains and the team checked the door, it was not locked. They went inside and saw rows of bunks with a bathroom at the end. The place had a small kitchen

to the right as you came in. Across from the kitchen area a computer was sitting on a desk with a phone alongside it. They started the computer and no one had put any security on it, so the team easily accessed the files. As they did, they found files with names of people. In one section they found a resource of information on the Remnant. In this were Constitutional documents, Bible scriptures, and more. But it was clear; these people were part of the Remnant. They quickly took some flash drive copies of the files. This would be invaluable to have and the Colonel would be pleased. In their hands were names, addresses, and other information of Remnant groups in the USA.

The team quickly left the area being sure to leave all things as they were. Back at the van they showed the Lieutenant what they had. He made copies on the system and sent them to the Colonel. Before long the Colonel called;

"Great work Lieutenant" the Colonel sounding happy "there is a lot of info and we are working on checking it out, but it does look real! Do not do a thing to these people. I don't want to tip them off that we know a thing. If we hit them tonight then this list will be useless. We must make plans to hit these all at once, so get back to our location. We will discuss the next move then." The Colonel stopped and waited for an answer

"Yes sir, will do; we will leave ASAP" finished the Lieutenant and then said, "Alpha 1 to Alpha base out"!

The Lieutenant hung up and it was in the pre early morning dawn that a large van and a black SUV could be seen alone leaving Livingstone. They would head to Billings and go down I25 and towards Denver.

Outside on the deck, the Reverend sat in chair relaxing as he checked his watch. It was eleven in the morning and the feeding of the livestock was done. Beside him sat a younger man and the two looked like they were enjoying each other's company. They had been discussing the meeting of the Remnant coming up. Similar groups to theirs would also be meeting. All of them had the same purpose and they worked hard to coordinate meetings. Many lives depended on them being held in secret and making sure everyone had all the latest information. This was to ensure that everyone was up to speed on events and information. There was much to cover for each member of each group, the information could save lives, even their own. These meetings were not taken lightly; everyone knew they faced an enemy who would never stop to destroy them. The Remnant was a small army in thousands of small cells in America. They were pro-constitution, pro-gun, pro-American, and many were Christians, but not all of them. But among the Remnant, as well; were Generals, judges, lawyers, soldiers, pastors, local political leaders, and many others. The people were of all races and they had one goal in mind, freedom and an America as it used to be. They saw themselves as the last bastion of defense against a modern world order that was dismantling America. As they sat there a familiar vehicle pulled up and he saw Gin driving, behind her was another vehicle with two men inside. They all got out and the Reverend rose to greet them.

"Hi Gin, glad to see you made it back" greeted the Rev

Glad to be back, we have had a couple of interesting days" Gin answered as Tiger came around the front of the car and stood by Gin. Paul hobbled around one side of the vehicle as Bruce; his arm in a sling opened a door and got out.

"You guys looked like you ran into trouble, you alright?" the Rev asked

"The Colonel's men Rev" answered Tiger as he looked back at Paul and Bruce who were waiting for Mac and Cliff to join them.

"Yes, there was trouble, we got through it, they won't bother us for a while!" answered Mac as he said "You must be the Rev, I am Mac; Tiger's uncle and I want to thank you and your people for helping out Tiger here." Mac finished and walked towards the porch

"Well Mac, no problem; it was Paul and Bruce here as you probably already know that saw the men troubling Tiger and helped him out!"

The Rev finished and called out, "bring some refreshments for our guests will you"

A voice from inside shouted out "We are already on it" and within moments there was a tray of sandwiches, fruits, salads, and drinks sitting on a table. Cynthia ushered the group over to the food. Everyone seemed to be hungry as they filled their plates, and then gathering on the porch took in the fresh morning air and good company.

"Gin", the Rev said suddenly "you recognize this young man, don't you? This is Tom"

"Yes, he is my contact in Jackson I was going to fill you in on it when I came back" Gin stopped and sipped her tea

"I figured you were, but there is something you don't know. Tom here has another job besides being your contact; he not only works with the Colonels, but as you can see; with us! He is what you call a double agent, but we are retiring him. He has been feeding us the bogus information that the Colonel gives him to give us. We then follow up through Tom funneling information back to the Colonel. Meanwhile, Tom tells us what is really going on with the Colonel and his men. The Rev stopped, then added "be ye wise as serpents

and harmless as doves"

Everyone chuckled, then Mac said, "so your being wise with this

double agent, how do you know he is not really working for the

Colonel and leading you on?"

"Well, the Rev said; He is my son. He has worked military

intelligence and was off the radar. We could not discuss his work

and because we did not want him to be involved, so we kept it hush,

hush! But Tom wants to help us and become more involved now that

he has finished his duty"

"I see" smiled Mac as he looked at Cliff, then added "It is my nature

to not trust people"

Cliff, looked around at everyone smiling and then agreed "That's

right"

"I finished some time ago giving the Colonel bogus info on one of

our Remnant groups." Tom stopped and looked at the Rev who

nodded with approval, and then he continued. "The group itself

volunteered to be uncovered to get the Colonel out in the open. So,

the group the Colonel got is a real to life Remnant group run by a

friends of ours; Bob and Tillie Owens. Finer people you will never find anywhere. He is a former military analyst, but his skills are much more. They called us and told us that they have the Colonels men recorded on hidden cameras taking info from the computer they had set up for them. Right now, the Colonel will be finding names, addresses, and locations of the Remnant. The names are all real, but what they don't know yet is that those names are people already on the governments kill list. The people mentioned are all volunteers and know what is going on. The locations however are past addresses. By the time they really figure out what is going on the Colonel will be in the open for us to hit. Our friends Bob and Tillie have already left the area and are at another location." Tom finished and looked around and everyone seemed pleased, except Mac and Cliff.

"It all sounds good Tom, and I know the Rev would not put his people in danger without truly knowing the costs; but look I know this guy and Cliff knows his type. The Colonel is shrewd, mean, and if there were anyone on earth to fear more, I do not know who it would be. He has always found out things, things that people don't want him to know. He gets the job done, he simply never misses" Mac stopped

Tiger looked at his Uncle and then at the Rev and spoke quickly "but Mac, he missed us and if he failed to get us, then he is not as unstoppable as he seems to be"

"That's right Tiger, the Colonel missed us because he was dealing with me, I know him and we were ready for him, but now there are so many unknowns. What about the entire Remnant group, can we guarantee their safety? The answer is no! I know it, Cliff knows it, and the Rev surely knows it"

"Mac, I do know and it has been taken into account, but we are in this battle to see it through. Our people, as do I and everyone on this Ranch know the cost. It is life and death, but Mac if we die; it is as scripture says, 'live or die, I am the Lords'" The Rev finished and saw Mac looking angry

"Rev" Mac shouted loudly; "I have heard that before and do you know how many of your kind, good believing Christians have died. I have buried them in Afghanistan, Iraq, Libya, Kenya, Nigeria, Indonesia, and in America. Rev what about the other scripture, have you told them it yet; it is found in Romans, which says 'for thy sake we are killed all day long, we are accounted as sheep for the slaughter'. Mac stopped, now visibly angered; he stomped off the porch to find a quiet secluded place. He did not like getting mad, but he has heard all this before from other well-meaning Christians and they all got themselves killed.

The Rev along with Gin and Tiger looked stunned as Cliff smiled and followed Mac. He knew Mac and understood full well why he said what he did.

"Rev, don't let my uncle bother you; he means well and he is very good at what he does" said Tiger

"What is it that your Uncle does Tiger, I mean that he does so well" The Rev asked right away

"Mac is good at killing people and staying alive, being able to go where most men would fear to go and he also knows what pure evil is. He has fought against it and been employed by people he has viewed as pure evil. The Colonel being one of those men" Tiger stopped and saw that Cliff had come back and overheard Tiger.

"That's right Rev, Mac is good at killing, staying alive, and knowing what pure evil is" Cliff stopped and rubbed his chin thinking a moment as everyone looked at him, then Cliff added "Rev I would trust this man with my life and I have on many occasions. You see, Mac left his former life and had put all this behind him until the

Colonel came after him. He was getting back to what he calls being 'a normal guy'. Now he has feelings he tried to put down, coming back. He is troubled by terrible dreams at night, and he gets night sweats from all his memories. He keeps it quiet from everyone, except from me" Cliff stopped and sipped his lukewarm coffee, with an "Ugh, cold" he sat it down

As the afternoon waned and the day continued, the group took the afternoon in stride and also Mac's words rang out in the ears of many. They know it is a battle, but had they bitten off more than they could chew. They were not professionals like Mac, Cliff, or the Colonel; but they were in this. How many had truly counted the cost and how many would make it through. Mac quoted it right and the scripture rang out in the ears of those who heard him "we are accounted as sheep for the slaughter".

The news rang out on the evening broadcasts "UFO watchers are celebrating tonight as the proof they have wanted has finally occurred. The latest in a series of massive UFO sightings has now ended. The first was in Israel where witnesses testify to a quantity of Silver saucer UFO's which hovered over the Dome of the Rock for some time and then simply vanished. With this were seen globes of small white lights in the hundreds that appeared on the Temple mount while reports of very tall large humanoid creatures being sighted in Israel with many relating the Nephilim accounts of Genesis Six. However, no one can explain these sightings but Israel is all abuzz over it. Then last week there were at least 20 UFO's which cruised over Phoenix. The crafts were clearly seen and were not military. This was a replay of the former Phoenix lights before, but this sighting was even more dramatic, happening in the daytime and at the noon hour rush. Witnesses are coming forward with first-hand accounts of tall beings over 8 feet or taller contacting them. Now last night we have another in the news with a sighting in Moscow. It again had many UFO's and a large mother ship. Outside of Moscow witnesses report that beings came out of one craft that were about 9 feet tall. Not much is known as the reason, but UFO watchers say that the massive sightings are proof that something big is going to happen soon." This is Amy Rogers for NFTV Europe signing off. With a click the monitor went silent.

Benjamin looked at the Prophet saying "see these appearances are happening all over"

"The Nephilim are alive and well and so are his devices to delude and deceive" said the Prophet and then he added. "These sightings and others will continue. These Nephilim are not alone, there are others and it is these who will indeed contact man and they will tell man that they are Gods come down to earth. These beings will say they made man and are back to help him move to the next level of awareness. The deception is moving forward and mankind who has rejected the 'Love of the truth' will be convinced to what they say as being true. But the fact is, the Nephilim, as well as these other beings will play a large role in the end of days." The Prophet stopped and headed outside. Benjamin knew it was time for the Prophet to be alone, as he did several times a day. Some days or even weeks on end he would be in seclusion seeking the Lord. The door shut behind the Prophet and Benjamin went to his desk and began working on his notes. His job was to provide a record of all the events going on. There was the Prophet and then his scribe Benjamin and this was his ministry. Ministry to the Prophet, just as Joshua ministered to Moses.

At another location deep at level thirteen, a monitor turns off and the General and the Colonel only smile at each other. Around them are a group of people dressed in long robes.

"It is going on as planned, it is going to be a grand day when Lucifer is finally revealed" The Colonel and the General clanged a toast of brandy and sipped it as everyone said "Hail Lucifer." Then as they finished their toasting, a large table, filled with all sorts of food for the guests was ready. They all poured over the delicacies, taking their favorites and then each one grabbed their favorite liquor and sat down. Soon the hall was filled with talking and beyond them a double door opened and as they sat there a figure came into the room. There was a bright light that seem to clothe him from head to foot. Accompanying him, one on the right and the other on the left were two very large angelic beings. They stood before the crowd and a glow came out from the center one who was dressed in a white business suit and tie. He had golden blonde hair which also radiated and looked at his guests smiling. At once the crowd arose and started chanting 'Hail Lucifer, Hail Lucifer, and Hail Lucifer' and as they quieted down he spoke.

"My friends it was a very long time ago when I walked up and down the stones of the throne of God. I knew him and soon realized that the God of Abraham was a liar. The truth is man did not fall into sin in the garden; but he was reborn into a newness of God himself. As man is now, God once was and as God is now, man will become. This is truth my friends. God does not want you to be like him, he is jealous; he says so in his own word! We will see man lifted up as Gods and thus the God of Abraham will be of no use." Lucifer stopped as people clapped and shouted their approval and then he began to speak again.

"We are almost ready for the chaos to begin. It will take over America and then the world. For the God of chaos to come, chaos must reign first. We have taken over principalities and our powers will bring the world together in peace and Godhood. We have our people in power right now from the Oval office of the United States to the U.N., and throughout the world. Let it come, let us be ready. I will ascend to the heights above God in the highest, for I am God; it has been written of this time and this hour by Daniel the prophet in chapter 7 of the Christians own bible which says of me; 'that horn that had eyes, and a mouth that spake very great things, whose look was stouter than his fellows. I beheld, and the same horn made war with the saints, and prevailed against them. And again, it says in the bible of the Christians Revelation chapter 13 of me; 'it was given unto him to make war with the saints and to overcome them; and power was given him over all kindred's, tongues, and nations. All that dwell upon the earth shall worship him.' The hour is coming shortly when the world shall worship me and you will reign with me, my friends; who see the light of Lucifer the God of all the earth" with that, Lucifer looked around at his two angels that stood beside him. They had been shining in a visible white light and by now drawn their swords as if ready to strike. Lucifer turned from them and looked straight at the crowd, saying "Let it begin, it has been given to me to make War, that through war, we will have peace. We will remove those instigators who have stopped the progression of my ascension and your destined Godhood."!

"Hail Lucifer, let that which is written be fulfilled, He shall reign and we shall reign with him, Hail Lucifer" the crowd getting louder now continued its chant of "Hail Lucifer" and as they spoke, Lucifer went back through the doors from whence he did come.

"That is what we are fighting for" said the Colonel

"That's right Colonel, that's right" agreed the General as the room silenced itself into small talk of admiration for their Lord who had appeared. As the night wore on, the celebration went on as well. The forces of light and darkness were gathered on a global scale and in the midst, was the Word of God which had to be fulfilled. The hour was close when the evil would be revealed as light to a rebellious world.

It was 6 pm and everyone had finished dinner and were now readying for the meeting. This was the group called Remnant and all over the country similar groups were meeting. The agendas had been given out and now it was time for the truth to be told. At the front was Gin who spoke up over the mic. The place was one of the outbuildings on the Rev's ranch and there were about eighty people sitting down.

"Greetings my friends" Gin spoke smiling and looking around "Welcome to this quarterly meeting of the Remnant. We do have first timers here; Stand up Tiger, Mac, and Cliff." The three got up and smiled looking around and then sat down. "You can get to know them after the meeting, if you have not done so already. We will have snacks and fellowship when we are done." Gin finished with

"The Rev is first up and then we will have a special word from Mac."

The Rev came to the podium and started to speak "Greetings my friends as our Lord said in John 15:20 'if they have kept my saying, they will keep yours also'; it is not just about a head faith", the Rev said pointing with this finger to the side of his head; "but one of keeping his word. We do the sayings; we keep the commandments as it says In Revelation chapter 14 'here are they that keep the commandments of God and the faith of Jesus'. We are to have faith as our Lord had faith and to keep the commandments according to his word. We are in that day and hour that the beast will be soon revealed and he will appear as light, Luciferian light to a world in chaos. We know chaos comes, we know why it comes; to bring in the god of chaos, Lucifer himself. He will wage war with us and he will overcome us according to scripture. But we will overcome him according to Revelation chapter 12, 'they overcame him by the blood of the Lamb, the word of their testimony, and they loved not their lives unto the death'". The Rev stopped to the loud cries of 'Praise and Amen' which came from the crowd and raising his hands towards heaven gave thanks. When it finally died down, he then continued.

"As much as we have succeeded, we have also lost comrades. They have passed into glory. Let us honor those in Alamogordo who lost their lives when the Colonel hit the group. I am afraid the group and the meeting place were betrayed by those within the group. King David knew very well of the treachery of man as did our Lord who was betrayed by Judas. David said of his experience in Psalm 55 'It was not an enemy who exposed me, defying me; it was thou, a man mine equal, my guide, and mine acquaintance. We took sweet counsel together and walked unto the house of God in company.' So, understand there will be people joining with us for various reasons, but although their words are honey, war is in their hearts. In all; twenty of our Remnant brethren were killed and as someone reminded me 'as sheep to the slaughter.' But we will continue and the battle will go on. We are not here to kill people, but to save souls. And in the process mend America so she can continue her free course. But we will defend ourselves. Need I remind anyone here that if Israel did not defend herself there would be no Jews in the Holy Land today? When they did not defend themselves, they died, as in Hitler's camps. Now another has come, he looks like Hitler, and he is Hitler for all intents, for war and bloodshed is in his heart. His allegiance is to the God of this world. Now I want to introduce Mac and let him speak. He has important things to tell us, Mac can you come forward?" The Rev looked at Mac and motioned for him to come up front. Mac arose out of his seat and stepped up on the platform and stopped beside the Rev. "I count it an honor to know this man and his nephew Tiger; whom many of you have met. He has been frank with us as we discussed the issues we face and for that I am grateful to him." The Rev stopped and shook Mac's hand and stepped aside as Mac took the mic.

"Hello everyone, I am new to your group; but I am not new to the Colonel or his kind. The battles we face are ones that mean life and death to many people. It is not just the death of the USA, but of many of our allies and the people within their borders. The plans for takeover are global, starting with America. This is a secretive group that was established before our nation was yet ten years old, a group formed to bring about a coup in this nation. But at that time, they could not finish it, they kept secret and those within became very rich and powerful. They worked to change the country from within and it was not until the 21st century that they had made enough headway to literally take over. Their power and heritage passed from Father to son, lineage to lineage, and generation to generation. They have succeeded in putting people in high places. They have connections from Pentagon to Wall Street to the Federal Reserve and the World Bank. They employ only the professional cold-blooded killer. They have carried out a covert war of intrigue and assassinations for many years. Remember President Kennedy, it was not Harvey Oswald alone or Jack Ruby by himself who killed the leader of the nation. It was a black op hit and planned from within the confines of this group. It is this group which the Colonel works for."

"Now the main base the Colonel works at is Alpha base. You might think he started it, but he did not. He was hired for his method of getting jobs done efficiently and secretly. Alpha base is an underground facility which has many floors. There is an elevator in the main house which takes you to the locations beneath. To illustrate the evil of this base let me tell you of level thirteen. It is filled with things that most people don't believe in, like demons, UFO's, Aliens, and Nephilim! I have been around them, seen them, and worked the area myself. I left some time back because I hated the agenda of these people. I wanted to be normal, to think normal things. There are things in level 13 that quite frankly if you saw these beings, well it would terrorize you. Believe me; these things are within this place for one purpose, which is the completion of Project Black light. Black light came out of the old Project Orion which was a way to propel spacecraft by nuclear explosions. You know Werner Von Braun who worked for Hitler, developing among other things like the V-2 rockets and later became head of NASA, well he supported this project along with Arthur C. Clarke. The original idea was created by Stanislaw Ulam a polish mathematician. Stanislaw contributed to the Manhattan project, but later had seen the viability of spacecraft propulsion through the means of nuclear explosions. Orion was created for that purpose and when President Kennedy made the goal of going to the moon, Orion was set to go ahead.

Problems of support and political intrigue killed Orion in 1964. But it became a black ops project with a bigger goal. This time it was a project for space exploration, space colonization, searching for extra-terrestrial life, and to create what was called the Dyson sphere, name after Physicist Freeman Dyson. The sphere was the catalyst of the project and it simply was a system of orbiting solar powered satellites which would encompass a star and had the ability to capture most or all of the stars energy. Our own orbiting satellites came out of Dyson's idea." Mac stopped and looked around the audience as he took a sip of water he had brought with him. "Now you all know of the history of area 51 and conspiracy theories, which many people call them. It was however, people like John Leer, Adam Sandler, Bob Lazzar, William Hynek and others that the credit goes for uncovering what was going on. Through their discoveries many in the world found out about area 51, secret projects, aliens, alien technology, UFO's, MJ12, and much more. Well those in the black ops wanted these things revealed because it took the heat off the real project. Soon Orion was remade into Project Black Light. It came after both the Canadian and American governments contacted alien entities. They could channel information in the beginning. What came out of that was Black Light. They would utilize technology of these beings for their free use of the planet, but with some restrictions. However, the project grew, the aliens were hard to control and some did not follow the path that Black light was preceding along. Some of these aliens were very bad characters and had a taste for blood, human blood. These were called the Nephilim by the scientists at the time referring to Genesis chapter 6. They were about 9 ft. tall or even taller, had a sloped forehead, and were part humanoid. Indeed, there was a battle with some of the aliens who were killed. In the process an agreement was made. That agreement was pursuing Project Black Light.

These people work to steel the darkness, that is make the darkness hardened or impervious to attack; simply put they will create a world of darkness. This would be a world with Lucifer as God; the God of this world. These people see Lucifer as the only one who understands men, and they work to bring about his kingdom. It would be an age of a new awareness, to make men gods, and to tear away the bonds that the God of Abraham had on the earth. So while it is evil and pure darkness, the world will see on the light of Lucifer who will be seen as God!

I will wrap this up by saying their goal is to reduce the earth's population. The will do this through wars, famines, pestilence, and plagues. These are things which they already have been doing. They manufacture the plague virus and they alone have the antidote. They produce weather changes to create drought and thus have food shortages. All this is done through technology, alien technology and human scientific advancement. They will create a one world government unlike anything before. These people see the day when Lucifer will be seen and will be god on this earth. They will fix the Jewish problem along with the Jerusalem problem. They will stop the Islamist problem as well. They will make war against Christians because they are the biggest threat to them. Project black light today is a very large program with multiple bases and technologies. Its political reach is at the highest levels of our government and its financing is limitless. If you were to kill the Colonel and destroy Alpha base, you would be just removing one tentacle of this giant octopus we call Project Black light.

Now let me mention another group which has been in a battle for supremacy of our nation that goes back to its beginning. I have worked for this group on and off for many years. Furthermore, I cannot divulge any information on it other than what I am now saying. But these people are blood kin to the people who founded this nation. It is made up of individuals, who like our forefathers want a constitutional government. They also are very powerful, very rich, and are as secretive as the others. They believe in the documents that were created at our inception. I was assigned to infiltrate the Colonel's group, which I did. But a mole in my own group at the highest levels relayed information about me to the other group. We found out about the mole and a contract was issued. The man was found one day with a heart attack in his apartment. My cover looked like it had been blown and before anyone could do anything, I was told to get out. I left the Colonel's base and my assignment ended. However, we expected them to come after me so we set up a dummy hideaway in Wyoming. It was then that Tiger and the others became involved and wound up at the ranch, through various circumstances.

I have given you enough right now." With that Mac finished and walked slowly to his seat.

The Rev sat there in silence for a moment thinking of all that was revealed, indeed this has deep roots. As Mac spoke the Reverend could literally see scripture after scripture being fulfilled. He thought to himself and then arose and said, "I stood upon the sand of the sea, and saw a beast rise up out of the sea", this is the beast that is rising as we speak. Friends we are one small cell among many cells in a body. We are made up of many people, faiths, beliefs, political persuasions, and abilities. This group is one of the Remnant believers in Jesus Christ; Yeshua ha Massiach. However, we welcome all people into our group. We have a common enemy who is destroying our nation and taking with it the Judeo-Christian roots it has had. For you and me our cause is for Christ and we know that the beast when he is revealed will make war specifically against those who 'keep the commandments of God and faith and testimony of Jesus Christ'. This my friends, is who we are! We are believers, we are Remnant, and we are ready for this battle."

The Reverend stopped as all eyes were on him, and then said, "let us take a break for now"!

The crowd seemed stunned with all the information and as the Reverend came down from the platform he was surrounded by people. The Rev was nice and shook hands, but as he did greet them; he would look around to find Mac in the crowd. He was not sure now, just whose side Mac was on. It was a lot of information, much too much information. But for now, he knew that in the end, the

Lord would be Lord overall, with the glory of the Lord filling the earth.

Chapter Six: Betrayal

The words of his mouth were smoother than butter, but war was in

his heart: his words were softer than oil, yet were they drawn swords

Psalm 55:21

Mac was sitting in a lawn chair in the shade of an old cottonwood

looking out at the rows of beets that were planted. He saw a hawk

circling overhead watching the ground for some food. A few cars on

the highway passed by now and then. The postal truck stopped at the

mailbox and put the flag down as he picked up mail from the ranch.

In a few moments, the road was clear and quiet. Mac was enjoying

the serenity as he heard footsteps behind him, then the voice of his

nephew called out.

"Last night was a good meeting Mac", said his nephew Tiger

"Yes, it was I just wished we did not have this battle Tiger. I have

seen too much blood and I am sick of it all. The killing never stops

and the spilling of blood continues. Then they had to go and kill

Melissa that was it. Now I am duty bound to avenge her, which I will

do" Mac stopped and thought deeply about her, then Tiger spoke.

"Mac do you remember when you and the Rev were talking and you quoted scripture, well that surprised me; I did not know you knew scripture and you seemed to quote it right or the Rev would have corrected you" He stopped and looked for an answer from his Uncle Mac.

"Yes Tiger, I did know it." Mac stopped and did not let any more information out.

"Well" asked Tiger questioningly

"Well what" answered Mac frustrated at the intrusion on his privacy

"Well tell me about it, How you came to know that scripture and what about all those Christians you talked about anyway" Tiger persisted and looked directly at Mac. Mac knew what Tiger wanted; his nephew was always asking questions. It was that inquisitive nature which got Tiger into this mess with the Colonel anyway. Mac guessed he came about it rightly.

"You won't give up on this will you Tiger" Mac looked back at him knowing the answer

"No Mac, I will pester you until I get the answer" Tiger smiled and saw his uncle weakening. Years ago, Mac would never have divulged it, but now Tiger saw the weary look on his Uncle's face and was concerned. "You look worn-out Mac"

"I am and I am equally tired of secrets as well" here is the story Tiger, get your pen and paper. Tiger stood there and did not go get his paper and pen, it was okay to listen; he would remember important details.

"Tiger it was years ago and I was much younger. I was an officer and worked black operations for the military around the world. We were a quick moveable force. The brass moved us around to hotspots where forces were threatening nations friendly to us. We had to go into Kenya and battle some rebels that had infiltrated out of Somalia. They were a hardened bunch and had many boy soldiers whom they conscripted. They had been slaughtering villagers living near the border, many of whom were Christians. They would come over the perimeter boundary line and raid churches, among other things. Then they would disappear back into Somalia. During those years of fighting our group killed many enemy combatants, but we also had made solid friends. We were brothers, close knit and among them was Cliff. We had bailed each other out, saved each other's lives countless times. But we also buried many comrades in all the assignments we had. These were young men, who died too early for a cause that really did not matter. But it mattered politically.

I also had another close friend. His name was Buddy. Buddy was a Christian; you know the quoting scripture all day kind of Christian. This guy was a Baptist and he knew his bible from one end to the other. We would discuss issues in the world, but Buddy would always bring it around to salvation." Mac stopped and as he did Tiger interrupted him saying "So you know all about salvation, then?"

"Well yes, mostly I guess. But I spent time in many nations, including that assignment in Kenya to persuade these Christians to leave. They would simply say 'if God be for us, then who can be against us'! One day we were on patrol and over the radio we got a call saying a church had been hit. We moved fast. We came to the border area and found the church; it was near a town called Mandera. Outside the church people were beginning to pick up the bodies. It was on a Sunday and right at ten o'clock when everyone was to be there, these rebels hit. They were from the same group we were told to hit. They went by Islamist theology and saw Christians as Infidels. So as we approached gunshots fired out and hit some of the people trying to pick up the bodies for burial. We dispatched some men and they hit the two snipers. It was quiet, so we posted lookouts and went inside. It was horrible, men had been disemboweled, women split open, the wooden cross was on some benches the people used and was smoldering. They had sat it on fire. The Pastor was hung up with a sign on his chest. It was stuck there with a large knife. Blood and guts were everywhere, men, women, and kids. It was horrible, all in the name of some god. I was angry and took the men and followed the group over the border. We caught up with them, some twenty soldiers including young boys. It was 4 am in the morning and they slept soundly. We hit hard, killing many and captured others. I was so mad I gutted the survivors and put a sign on their chests saying, "cross over again and this will be you". I took their guts and spread them across the roads. I had gotten vengeance. The problem was my friend Buddy, who was the Christian, he was angry at me. He saw the devil in me, he said. He was right, I was mad as hell and the devil was in me. I did to these men as they did to the Christians. I took vengeance for the innocent ones I saw. Later Buddy and I sat down and I challenged him on this. He would not budge, it was one thing to defend yourself and the innocent, it was quite another to kill and torture your prisoners. He took me through scripture and the final one he gave me was the one in Romans I quoted, 'we are led as sheep to the slaughter'! I was mad and we fought, nearly coming to blows over the situation. The next day I did not speak to him. I hated him for the hypocrisy of it all. We were patrolling back from the border towards the small town where the church had been hit. I had a scout out front and one in back. I was towards the front when gunfire erupted from the front and two sides. We looked trapped, my men out front went down, and then I got hit. As I sat there, bleeding two men came at me firing. I knew this was it; I began to feel faint, but kept firing. It was them or me! It was then that Buddy jumped in front of me firing as he did so and the two went down. But Buddy had been hit several times; he lay on me where he had fallen trying to protect me. Before I could speak a word; he died. You see Tiger, I do know scripture, more than you would think. I regret now my actions and those things I said to my best friend Buddy. But as I looked around Cliff was also hit. We called for an evac and we all left to go back to the main base. Both Cliff and I healed up and finished our tour. We do not talk about it, but he knows full well why I can quote some scripture." Mac finished and as he did, Tiger came to him and gave his uncle a hug, with a tear in his eye he said, "I am sorry Mac for pushing you on this".

"It is okay Tiger, but even today it still hurts. If I had it to do over again, I am afraid I would still go after those men and do to them what they did to those Christians, this is what still worries me Tiger" Mac finished and looked back out at the field. Tiger saw Mac turning to look away and he quietly moved back to let his Uncle have some more quiet time. As Mac sat there, he fondly remembered Buddy and then before he could catch himself, he said out loud "Buddy, I am sorry pal." The evening sun was going down as Mac finally realized how long he had been thinking of everything he had told Tiger. Times go fast and so did this day, with that Mac went inside.

The Colonel stood over the shoulder of the communications officer and looked around the room. Here was command central for Alpha base and they were now coordinating their covert strikes against those on the list found in the Montana compound. "Lieutenant, have you sent your men into the compound there?" asked the Colonel impatiently as he also waited for others to check in. They were simultaneously hitting numerous targets around the country.

"Yes Colonel, the team is in place now." The Lieutenant finished speaking quickly and then answered a call from his men. "Sir there is no one here, the computer is also gone. We are going to sweep further into outlying areas for other underground shelters." The voice stopped and waited for a confirmation. After a short recon of the area, the team searching the Ranch had found nothing. The Sergeant called the Lieutenant.

"Go ahead Sergeant" answered the Lieutenant and then he got on the com with the Colonel "Sir the place is empty, seems they cleared everything out.

"Well Lieutenant go forward with operation pitchfork; do you have all the stuff to plant on the place?" ask the Colonel

"Yes sir, we have the ammunitions, bullets, guns, grenades; more than enough to convince the people this was being prepared for terrorism in the United States. We will also plant the drug stash as well, we will precede Sir." The Lieutenant finished

"Lieutenant, I also want you to plant explosives around the place. It will look like these guys booby-trapped the place. That will really

get the Feds mad at our targets. I have other reports coming in,
seems like those places are empty; the addresses are out of date I
suspect. The names however are real; we already have them on our
lists. I will proceed with our track down. Lieutenant as soon as
you're done call the Feds with the tip on this place and let them take
care of it from there." The Colonel finished and thought for a
moment forgetting that the Lieutenant was signing off

"We will do Colonel, out!" The lieutenant finished and looked out
the van. He had more equipment and men, than the first time he was
here. They were all gathered around as he said:

"Proceed with pitchfork and make it be quick, also you know how to
stash the drugs, make sure no one can see you, then clean up, leave
no traces. We must leave quickly".

Within a short time, the Ranch, outbuildings, and main house was
packed with all the right evidence to convince anyone, including the
Feds of the criminal nature of the Ranch and those who owned it.
The Lieutenant made a call on his secure untraceable phone to the
Feds, detailing the Ranch as a potential terrorist stronghold. Under
the cover of the morning, the unmarked vehicles took out and left the
area.

"Sir we have the hit teams, six teams of two each. They will dispatch the people on the list and then report back." The security officer, named Zee stood at attention looking at the Colonel behind his military green metal desk. It looked like it had come out of the Vietnam era and beside the desk was a large four drawer metal file cabinet that looked as bad as the desk.

The Colonel looked up and said; "Good work Zee, who did you put on these hits?"

"Well sir, we have a group just back from Argentina. They are the Mortiphilim sir. These guys are big, powerful, and will not stop. They have a perfect kill record." As he was speaking they were interrupted. Turning around the Security officer saw the leader of one of the hit teams. He was very tall, wearing a business suit, tailored to fit. He had long hair, dark sunglasses to hide his eyes, and had an auto strapped to his side. His large boots made noise as he came into the room. These are direct descendants of the Nephilim, but they have through the ages evolved into a more humanlike appearance, with a little help of the transgenic program that they have at the base. There are still the other species of Nephilim out there; these are not tamed so to speak, and look much like the legendary Bigfoot species. These Mortiphilim are tame to some extent, but they need to be controlled always. They keep to themselves and are not at all interested in the many things humans are. As he came closer, he spoke up:

"Noah talk to Colonel"

"Yes, Noah; what can I help you with", the colonel answered getting up and looking at him

"Colonel no want people live? Noah Kill people, so Colonel no take care of them." Noah asked

"Yes, Noah you kill people, make sure they never see daylight again" The Colonel finished and turned to look out the window.

"No daylight for People Colonel, Noah understand" Satisfied, Noah turns around and leaves. The hard thump, thump of Noah's boots was only covered by the hard slam of the door.

"Noah, it is quite a name, huh Zee?"

"Yes sir, it was indeed someone's joke or insight that led them to name him Noah." Zee stopped and waited for a moment.

"You can go now Zee, keep on top of them will you and keep me updated daily; I want those on that list dead and I want it done quickly. And Zee, be sure to put Mac's name at the top of the list as well; but bring him back alive, you hear me Zee? I want Mac here alive, even if he is barely alive; we can patch him up. I have plans for him! You are to make sure Noah and his teams don't go around just killing anyone they feel like. I don't want another incident like the last time where they killed a whole company of policemen in South America in order to get a hit finished." The Colonel quieted down

"Yes sir, I will keep track of them and any trouble like that we will bring them in. Plus, I will take a special team with me to go get Mac", the security officer saluted and went out not waiting for a salute from the Colonel.

The Colonel heard the door close and as he gazed out his window the calm of the desert lay before him. He loved this view and as he stood there he thought of Noah and his kind. Most people knew of these entities as Nephilim. Noah and his kind were perfect killers. They were frightening to many who saw them. They had perfect vision at night; it is no wonder that at night is when they do all their hunting. Their sense of smell is extraordinary and can smell anything that approaches them from a long distance. Their hearing is also very good, but in the end these creatures have a taste for blood. Human blood, they kept vials of it at level 13 where Noah and his kind stay when not in use. A little fresh blood helps keep them calm. But the history of the Nephilim is that they like human flesh. Although very terrifying, they could be killed, the bible is proof of that. Both Joshua and Caleb cleaned out the promised land of the older Nephilim. The new generations of Nephilim that they call Mortiphilim are adapted to modern human society and do quite well living out their lives as humans in the big cities. Noah and his group were trained to do what they do. They had a natural instinct for the cold blood nature of killing humans. But most of the new breed has learned to develop the tastes and natural cravings in the human environment. They are also able to pro-create with humans. They do fear man, because it was man who almost succeeded in extinguishing them from the planet. For the most part humans live with the Mortiphilim and the Pleiadeans on a daily basis. Someone passing them in the street would never know it. But one fact is sure, these live in the large cities where they can blend in and no questions are asked, because in the end they do live with a secret.

Gin was heading home and Tiger decided to come along. They had both agreed that a little time of relaxation and possibly fishing would be great. They had left the Rev's early in the morning before many would notice. Gin was about home now and was pointing to some places they could go and relax. They wanted to get away from all the problems, fighting, and troubles caused by the Colonel. Gin pulled into her driveway and got out. She and Tiger went up to the house and as they got close the smell of fresh baked bread wafted like a thick cloud around the open screen door. They both went in and Gin's mom was in the kitchen.

"Mom, I'm home and I brought a friend" spoke Gin looking for her mother as she walked into the kitchen by the sink. She went over and gave her a hug. Her mother looked at her lovingly and then spoke: "Gin dear, your friend can sleep in the guest bedroom".

"Yes, I thought so, but wanted to ask, we are also going to go camping and fishing; can you come?" Gin stopped and saw Tiger looking out the big picture window.

Tiger turned around and walked to Gin and her mother, "Hi Gin's Mom, I am Tiger, that is my nickname; so I stick with it. Billy Ames is my real name".

"Hello Billy Ames, I am Mary Engle; Mom to you and Gin" Mom Engle looked at the two standing there and thought a nice-looking couple. Billy was a couple inches taller than Gin and had dark brown hair to his collar. She couldn't help but think of a godly man for her Gin to marry and now she wondered if Tiger was a Christian or not. Tiger followed Gin out of the kitchen, through the double doors to the patio. Both Ma and Pa, a pair of Aussie shepherds greeted the two; especially Tiger as if they had known him all along. Shortly, Gin's mom brought out ice tea and glasses for them all. Then she returned and came back with bread, butter, and honey. The three sat around the redwood table and munched on the snacks.

"Gin, honey I am afraid I cannot go with you two. I have some meetings lined up with those in the church and cannot call them off. We have an extra tent and sleeping bag for Tiger, you two will have a great time. Take dad's fishing stuff and get a day license at the lodge. It won't be long before you guys will be eating fresh trout by the campfire in no time." Gin's mom stopped and looked at both of them, then said "you two look so good together, I just..." Then she stopped

"Mom, stop it" Gin urgently shot in, she was embarrassed and knew her mom couldn't help being the matchmaker, she knew her mother wanted a husband for her and grandchildren that would come later.

Gins mother seemed oblivious to the plea to 'stop it' and continued;

"It is just you too look good together"!

Tiger saw the talk going on and felt a little out of place. He liked Gin but not marriage. His thoughts were on beating the Colonel, not marital bliss. One day, though, thought Tiger; 'a nice woman as a wife would be great'. He looked at Gin and the sun was now shining through a sunroof in the patio that set her hair and face aglow in the golden rays. She had a great look, was smart, and a great personality. Gin saw Tiger look at her and she smiled "Tiger we will go to the Big Horns, it is some drive; but you will love it"!

"Great, I do want to get out and away as this last month or so has been a busy one" Tiger finished and took a piece of the bread, put on honey and ate it.

The afternoon went well as the day past into night and the quietness of the small town took over. The three of them had moved to the front lawn and were now watching the summer night sky. It was filled with myriads of stars. The Milky Way made a path through the heavens as a shooting star hit the farthest horizon. It was peaceful and far away from the dangers of the Colonel, or so it seemed tonight. Gin took it all in and was thoroughly enjoying both Tiger and her mother's company.

The Rev was sitting in his favorite chair and reading the newspaper. The statewide newspaper was popular and covered the sparsely populated state. If something happened in the small state, the newspaper would have it. It was a daily habit to read it slowly but surely with a cup of coffee especially in the winter time or ice tea in the hotter months. As he sat reading Mac and Cliff came into view and over the top of the newspaper, the Rev looked up as Mac spoke. "Rev we have enjoyed your hospitality and we will be in touch. Right now, we must scope out the Colonel and his men to find out their next moves. If your right about the info you let him have with that raid in Montana then he will be on top of it." Mac finished and saw the Rev's worried look.

"You look heartsick" Mac said of the Rev as he looked up with panic in his eyes

"I am sick, very much so. This article says here that the Feds busted a terrorist ring and as they did many them got killed. Seems like a hot tip turned into a booby trap for some of the men. They recovered guns, ammo, c-4, and other ammunition as well as drugs." The Rev

finished for a moment and Mac spoke up

"Let me guess Rev, it was your Montana sanctuary; right?" Mac

finished, now with a worried looked, he saw the Rev was indeed

deeply moved by this.

"Yes, your right Mac, and get this, it says they have leads on the two

main leaders, one of whom is a former military analyst with the

Pentagon" The Rev stopped and looked up

"Is that your man their speaking of?" Cliff asked

"Yes, it is I am sure of it. Bob was a military analyst for 25 years. If

they are on the run what's the chance that they will get away?" The

Rev Stopped

 "Rev, these guys don't play fair and they have all the connections"

Cliff pleaded

"Before we were just battling the Rev and now we wind up battling

the Feds as well; how can anyone escape that?" asked the Rev"

"Normally Rev a person would not have a chance" answered Cliff

"Listen Rev, you guys trust your God, right? Then they will get

away, possibly with his help. But Rev this is the standard operating procedure for the Colonel, huh Cliff?" Mac looked at Cliff who nodded affirmatively and said "Yes"

"I had better get the word out to all the groups, we must get Bob and Tillie to safety" The Rev stopped as the phone rang. The Rev picked up his cell and answered "Hello"

"Rev this is Squire Dickens; I'm calling to let you know that as you probably have already read about the raid on the Montana compound. The Feds are after Bob and his wife. The news just came up and said they found them. They are both dead after a firefight. Our sources in the morgue said the bodies were taken out and were in pieces, covered over with sheets spotted with blood. They said a Policeman on the scene who found the bodies told them 'it looked like a slaughter house in that hideout of theirs, but the one weird thing, most of the blood had been drained from the corpses'. They also will not release that several other bodies were found as well. Rev, you know Bob and Tillie were staying at a Remnant location out of Idaho springs did you not, will that is where they hit and where the slaughter took place." The Rev went pale, his brow was sweating and his heart began pounding. Fear fell and sadness hit all at once. He put up the phone with a weak "thanks I will get back to you" and then just stared at both Mac and Cliff.

Mac knew that look as did Cliff. "What's going on?" Mac asked

"They are dead, both Bob and Tillie along with the Remnant group where they were staying. Squire Dickens that is his codename; said our sources in the Morgue confirmed all this by saying that 'the bodies were in pieces, slaughtered or so it looked like. Plus, the bodies had virtually no blood left in them; it had been drained! It was horrible and they never seen this type of thing before.'" The Rev finished and asked, "Mac what are we up against really?"

Mac and Cliff both looked shocked and they both sat down in the nearest chairs. They knew death, they knew blood, and unfortunately, they also knew there was only one thing that could do this. Both Mac and Cliff looked at each other and said to the Rev

"The Colonel's special hit team"!

"What do you mean?" asked the Rev

"Nephilim, giants, Genesis Six Rev; you know the stuff don't you! Do we have to paint a picture here?" Mac replied softly and he could feel anger boiling up inside him.

"Nephilim, yes I know them, or of them in Chapter six of Genesis. When the Sons of God came into the daughters of men, their offspring became the Nephilim or Giants in those days. Some became the mighty and renowned men in those days; but soon they began to kill humans. They were so evil after a while that God destroyed them along with the other humans of that day for the evil they did." The Rev Stopped

"Well Rev, not all of them died, because as you and I both know the Israelites fought and conquered them. Some of them left the Holy Land before Israel came against them. The giants who fought with Israel ended up dying." Mac explained as he thought more about what had happened.

"But these are special; they are the offspring of the offspring and the product of transgenic changes. The result is that they have become more human looking. Project Black light trained some, like Noah, the leader of the Colonel's hit men. They are killers, and almost nothing can stop them. They are perfect killing machines. Once sent for you they will not stop until they finish their job. The blood also is drained off by these guys who drink the stuff like you and I drink ice tea. They also like human flesh. I guess if you believe they are from fallen angels then you can also believe it is in their nature to be so evil because they rejected the good." Mac stopped and quieted down, then said "this puts the fight up a notch; I will have to make some calls"

"Mac what should I tell the groups, how can we stop them and who else are they going for?" asked the Rev

"Well, they probably are part of the Colonels plans to make all your groups look like terrorist cells and then he will send his hit teams after the names on your list! The salting down of your Montana place with c-4 and also booby traps was a stroke of evil genius. This way even the Feds will believe all you have out west are terrorist cells. By doing this, he makes it easy for the government, especially the President who also is in this with the Colonels group to declare martial law." Mac again stopped, he had done way to much talking lately, he did not like it; but both the Rev and his people needed help; but first Mac needed some more men.

"Look Rev I am going to get some more men to help us, can any of your people fight? We will be fighting covertly until the civil war erupts, which is what the Colonels group wants. Until the real fighting starts, we need to train and get ready. But believe me Rev;

you are not in this alone!" Mac finished and then said, "Rev we will
be in touch, we must get going"

"Mac, indeed we do have men who will fight, we will wait for your
word. But what do I tell the groups and those on the list?" the Rev
Stopped

"Tell them to be careful, the hit teams always strike at night, put up
lights; lots of lights, they hate them; then get big guns and aim for
the brain. But Rev." Mac stopped short

"Yes Mac, go on" The Rev urging him to continue

"Pray Rev, pray like you guys have never prayed before that your
God will deliver you out of this hell" Mac finished and with Cliff at
his side went out the door.

The Rev sat there half sick and much too tired. His wife had been
listening and now was in tears. She came over and hugged her
husband of 40 years. Together they wept softly, caressing each other,
comforting each other, and calling on their God to intercede. As they
did, a peace came over them and the Rev felt a voice in his heart
saying, "Trust me, I am Alpha and Omega and I am in charge here".

After a short trip to the local gas station and to buy some snacks
for their trip to Cliff's, they were on their way. The Sun was now

behind the horizon and in the dusk of the evening the long road

stretched out ahead. Cliff was driving Macs truck that they had

come to the Rev's in. Mac was now on his secure sat phone.

"Yes sir, they have the hit teams out and they are already making a

mess of these people. This Remnant group doesn't stand a chance

against these killers." Mac stopped, then added "no sir I did not tell

them they had no chance, it would not have made a difference. I told

them to trust in their God." Mac stopped and listened quietly "I

know you don't believe in God sir, but it will help them and also our

side. I need you to send me my team; they need to be ready to hit

covertly sniper style. We will have to make this work sir; I don't

want these innocent people killed." Mac listened as the voice got

louder, then it quieted down; Mac once again spoke up "I know sir

many innocent people will die, but I can do something about this,

these are good Christian Patriots. Yes sir, we are heading back to

Cliffs, we will relocate to our winter base in time." With that, Mac

hung up.

As they drove along the road, a few cars passed them. They both

enjoyed the peace and comfort of this country and by now the night

had fully displayed its curtain of stars and galaxies. Then they came to a well-lit section of the interstate with an exit to the right. Before the exit they noticed something in the road ahead. Cliff slowed to a crawl and rolled down his window for a better look. Mac also looked out his window as he grabbed his pistol, and then a shot rang out and the glass splattered all over. Mac looked over and a saw Cliff leaning over the steering wheel, he had been hit. Mac immediately grabbed Cliff, and another shot rang out and he felt pain, then he lost grip of the wheel and the whole vehicle ran through a fence and flipped in a field. The car was still running and the smell of gas wafted through the night air. Mac was semi-conscious and Cliff was nowhere to be seen. He must have been thrown clear.

Mac was drifting in and out of consciousness as he smelled a horrid stench and heard people coming. The English they spoke was broken and not very clear. Immediately Mac thought "Nephilim", and as he fought to grab his gun, he did not know where he was. Suddenly a voice erupted.

"That's him, the Colonel wants him alive" grab him and we will get him back fast, I called in a copter.

"What about the other one? Can we have him?" A voice questioned

"No leave him alone, we are not to touch him, besides after the last hit; the Colonel was mad. We made too much of a mess of it all."

"Well we got the job done did we not? The voice replied

Mac lay there as two strong hands gripped his legs and two more his arms. He could barely make out any words, and then he heard the whop, whop, whop of blades. It was the copter coming to bring them back to base. This had been a night hit and their source inside the Rev's had told them correctly. The deal had been made, Mac for the Group.

As the night passed midnight the Alpha base came into view. The copter touched down inside the compound. Men from within the house came out with a stretcher and put Mac on it. Mac was now unconscious and they could have easily killed him. But this was the Colonels turf and his idea is never to make death easy, but to make it work for you. The Colonel would lead Mac through hell and in the process either bring back on board or kill him slowly. He will make Mac regret the day he saw the base or the Colonel.

Looking out the window, the Colonel saw the copter and Mac was now on a stretcher. He would be taken to their secure area and the sick bay. Doctors there would nurse him back to health and then,

Mac would be sent to level 13. It would be there that Mac would find the real pain. The Colonel smiled as he called the General.

"I know general that you wanted Mac dead, but opportunity availed itself and we took advantage of that. Yes, sir we got him, he is wounded, but not dead", The Colonel was happy and it echoed in his voice

"I am glad for both our sakes Colonel. Now do what you do best and get the job done with Mac once and for all." The General stopped and was visibly happy, he took out one of his Cuban cigars and lit it up, and then he walked over to his bar and poured himself a celebration drink. It was a fine night he thought, yes, very fine indeed and with that he blew a ring of smoke out and smiled.

Chapter Seven: Meet the Master

I will ascend above the heights of the clouds; I will be like the most

High Isaiah 14:14.

Tiger had just sat down with his breakfast of brook trout rolled in cornmeal and fried crisp. He and Gin had caught them early in the morning on the lake. He also had fried potatoes and some hot camp coffee to wash it all down with. Gin came and sat close by Tiger. The fire was filled with red hot coals and the coffee pot was sitting close to the fire, but not in it. As the two sat in the chairs they had brought with them, the pines above moved gently with a mid-morning breeze. It was about nine am and the air was a bit chilly at this altitude. Birds called camp robbers came and flew into the area around Gin and Tiger looking for scraps. Squirrels were busy scampering around the camp sites, as people were packing up to go. They had been staying in a popular Camp ground in the Big Horns and close by were several streams and a big lake. The local lodge there was very busy and later the two had planned on going there to have some dinner in the restaurant. It was a beautiful old lodge with big logs forming the walls and roof; with all of that sitting upon a concrete foundation. In the center of the restaurant was a huge round fireplace with native rock forming a ledge around the pit. The chimney rose straight up through the log roof and the smell of pines burning wafted in the mountain air throughout the valley where the

Lodge sat. The whole area was ringed with peaks, ledges, and forests with the lake in the center and meadows stretching out from the lake to the ridges beyond. The lodge also had camp sites but Gin and Tiger chose to stay a couple of miles away in the campground near South Fork. There were also small cabins for rent on the lakeshore as well. Indeed, it was a well-placed area for those who wanted to enjoy a slice of God's country. The whole area was full of both white tail and mule deer, plus Elk roamed the area. Coyote and Mountain Lion, along with many other critters were common to the region.

Tiger looked at Gin as she swallowed her last bite of food. She took a gulp of coffee and wiped her mouth. She was a pretty gal, he liked that they were friends. Gin saw Tiger watching her and said "What"? "Oh, I was just thinking about this area, how pretty it was?" said Tiger, with a lump in his throat, covering up for the real thoughts he was having concerning Gin. No doubt he was attracted to her! "Yes, it is great isn't it" Gin finished and then looked at the cars passing by. The campground was emptying for the day with only a few campers left. By the night, the place would again be full. Gin had booked this campsite in advance before they left.

"Gin, I want to know more about your faith and the Rev, I want this religion" Tiger finished and looked anxious.

"First Tiger, I don't have religion. Religion is an institutionalized system of beliefs and it can be from any deity or god or system of worship men want. The bible speaks of Belial, Baal, Ashteroth, and the Queen of heaven. Israel got mixed up in all of this by serving other gods, but they also tried to serve the God of Israel. This did not work, the True and living God won't work with Evil; he can't. To bring Israel back to the one true God, prophets were sent to warn Israel, but the people would not listen so they were judged. The bible says that "there is a way that seemeth right unto man, but the end thereof is death!" Gin looked at Tiger as he spoke up

"Really, its not religion? I always thought I was a pretty good person. I mean compared to all those killers and even the Colonel, I am a saint" Tiger stopped

"Well Tiger it is written, all have sinned and come short of the glory of God. Men are not sinners because they sin; they sin because they are sinners. See the difference; we are sinners and it is in our nature to sin or go against God. People think they are sinners because they sin or do something wrong, like murder. But the reality is God accepts men as they are, if they will come and repent. There is no reason for men to die and go to hell. God sent his son, John 3:16 tell us "For God so loved the world that he gave his only begotten son that whosoever believes in him would not perish but have eternal life"!

"Well I believe in him, I know that verse" Tiger looked at Gin puzzled

"Tiger that word believe is not like the American word to simply have a head belief, this word has action; it implies to believe upon, trust in, and cling to. It is like a life preserver. If you are in the ocean and your boat sank and you were in the water, you would drown if you didn't find help. You look around and see a life preserver and say to yourself 'I believe that life preserver will save me', but if you do not go to it, put it on and cling to it; that preserver will do you no good. This is just like that Tiger, you must put on the Lord Jesus. In John chapter one it says of the Lord "he went to his own and his own received him not, but to as many as did receive him; to them gave he the power to become the sons of God. Even to those who believe in his name, that is 'Trust in, Cling too, and rely upon' him. In John chapter three again it says we must be 'born again of the Spirit'. It is a spiritual rebirth, where we repent, receive him, and walk in his ways as he walked. John chapter three also says that many do not come to the Lord, because they love darkness. When you come to the light, it exposes your sins and when you repent and follow him; you have fellowship with him and his blood cleanses you from all sin." Gin stopped and saw that Tiger looked lost

"Man, I did not know it was so difficult to understand and to do, how can I be saved? I don't know any of this?" Tiger finished and he felt confused and worried, something inside of him was moving him. He felt differently, like a light had shone on him.

Gin looked at Tiger and grabbed his arm, getting his attention.

"Look Tiger, it is easy. Salvation is free. It is discipleship that is the cost. Do you want to know God the Father and his Son?"

"Yes, sure I do, but how?" Tiger replied

"Well, Jesus Christ is the English name for the Lord. His shortened Hebrew name is Yeshua Ha Massiach. He was born of a virgin, a Jewish woman by the name of Mary. She married Joseph who became his earthly father. When he was Thirty years old, he went out to proclaim officially that he was the Messiah of Israel. He fulfilled all the law and prophets. He went to his own people first; he was the 'Consolation of Israel'. His own priests, Pharisee's, and many of the people rejected him. He rose up 12 apostles to carry his word, and a following of the people believed on him. He was brought before the High Priest and later before the Romans. He was condemned to die on the cross. The scripture says, 'cursed is anyone who is hanged on a tree'. On that day, Jesus was crucified on the cross and became sin, a curse for us. He was sinless, yet he took upon himself our sins, and shed his blood. He was dead and then buried in a Tomb and three days later he arose from the dead. He was seen alive of the Apostles, many witnesses, even as many as 500 at once. He left instructions for the church and ascended to heaven in a cloud. Two angels stood by and saw the apostles standing there, and they said 'ye men of Galilee why stand ye here gazing; this same Jesus will come again in like manner as ye have seen him go'! When we receive Christ, we believe these things to be true. You see Revelation 12:11 confirms to us that 'we overcame by the blood of the Lamb, the word of our testimony, and we love not our lives unto the death'. Tiger what I am telling you is part of my testimony. Receiving Christ is to believe in your heart that he died on the cross for your sins and that God our Father raised him from the dead, and he now stands at the right hand of the Father and is coming soon. This is overcoming by the blood of the Lamb. Jesus is the Lamb of God, the Passover Lamb, and fulfilled the Day of Atonement. I said all of that to tell you, simply believe that he died for you on that cross that he was dead and then was resurrected, and is at the right hand of the Father and coming again. Receive this truth into your heart that he died for your sins! Scripture also says in 1st John 1 that if 'we sin we can confess our sin, God is faithful and just of forgive us of that sin'. Ask Jesus to come into your heart and ask his forgiveness Tiger; the Spirit of God will come into you and you will be born again by the Spirit." Gin looked at Tiger and he held out his hand. Gin took it and they prayed together.

"God, I believe your son, Jesus Christ died on that cross for me. I am a sinner and I ask you to forgive me. Come into my heart and live, fill me with your Spirit and help me to understand you more so I can walk in your ways." Tiger finished, and he felt at peace, a joy seemed to well up in him and a tear came to his eye. "I have never felt this, I feel funny Gin"

"That is your rebirth, the Spirit of God. Romans chapter 8 tells us that the 'Spirit itself beareth witness or confirms with our Spirit that we are the children of God" Gin stopped and looked back at Tiger, handing him a present, saying "Here is a gift I brought for you, it is a bible and some tapes by the Rev. They will help you to start your new life in Yeshua. We have a couple more days here, let's fish, camp, and study Gods word. We need to prepare you for what comes; this includes God's marching orders for the last days in which we live." Gin stopped

"Gin, thanks a lot; I was not a church going person and I grew up with a single parent. My mother worked hard and raised me as good as she could. I never knew my dad. We never knew of Salvation but we believed in God and knew of Jesus; but never personally. It was a matter of surviving daily and mom battled to put food on the table, pay the bills, and raise me right. We would even go to church from time to time but no one, not even the Pastor spoke of Salvation. But I have always thought on God and wanted to know him better. I knew I was missing something; but until now, I just never knew what it was!" Tiger quit talking and quickly gave Gin a hug saying again "Thanks Gin, you have helped me a lot."

Gin accepted the hug and tears came to her eyes. She felt good, Tiger needed to hear the truth of the gospel and she was glad the Lord had prepared his heart to receive the saving truth within it. Tiger backed away and shook off the remaining tears saying, "I have never cried so much, now about that fishing, I believe that I have to catch a few trout today." He smiled and took a gulp of his now lukewarm coffee; but it tasted fine this day; yes, in his world; now it was just fine.

Gin too felt good this day but she knew the challenges for Tiger and all believers everywhere in these last days. She felt a stirring in her spirit like something was wrong; but did not let on to Tiger; who was by now grabbing the fishing gear to take to the lake.

As Gin strode alongside Tiger to the lake shore, she thought this day that Tiger had truly met the Master; but there is another one, a serpent, the father of lies, the beast who is coming. He will bring a delusion with him and present himself as "light" and in so doing many will want to "Meet the Master". That is, the "Master of sin and delusion". Gin shook off these thoughts. Thoughts for another time and another place but for today Gin would enjoy the day with her friend.

The two of them smiling and chatting walked down the path to the lakefront. The sun was shining and the pines had a welcoming sound to them. The grass and meadows were glorious in their colors and they both knew that today, for them; God was indeed on the Throne and his Son was coming soon!

Cliff looked around the room. A curtain was pulled all around his bed and he was hooked up to a machine which monitored his pulse and other signs. He had a clear bag filled with some watery looking solution that dripped into the long tube going into the vein in his arms. His bed was propped up slightly and the room was quiet. Cliff tried to move and immediately pain shot through his body. Somebody had his ribs taped and his arm had a bandage around it. His whole body felt terrible. He tried to get up but fell back into the bed. Soon the curtain opened as he tried to move.

"Don't move, you will pull out the stiches. Here I will grab a mirror and you can look yourself over", the nurse attending him spoke with authority and Cliff immediately stopped moving.

Cliff looked at himself in the mirror. His eyes were black and blue; he had a bandage around his head. His face was scarred as were his arms. His face looked swollen and not at all like who he was.

"Who are you and where am I at" Cliff asked her

"You are in the hospital and I'm Nancy. I will be your nurse and

Tom will be your aide today. What is your name? Asked Nancy

"Cliff Burrows, a rancher; what happened?" Cliff asked but then also

added "I had a friend with me, have you seen him?"

"No one else was around the scene, just you. You had been thrown

from the vehicle. Didn't anyone ever tell you to wear your seat belt?

Your ribs are bruised and will be sore for some time. Someone shot

at you. They hit you to the right of your heart, near the shoulder, in

the muscle, no vitals hit; but you will be sore for some time. We

pulled the bullet out and the Sheriff has it. They will want to ask you

questions. By the way, your truck was totaled. You are lucky to be

alive. Now here, take these pills and drink this stuff. When you can

get out of bed we will take the catheter out. You have been in a coma

for a couple of days. You hit your head very hard and had a

concussion. I have got to make my rounds; the doctor will be around

in the morning early, he can answer your questions." Nancy watched

Cliff take the pills and drink the mixture she had prepared for him.

She gave him the menu and instructed him on ordering his

preferences for meals.

Cliff watched her leave the room and soon the aide came in.

"Hi, I am Tom, your aide, do you need anything?" "Not now" Cliff answered. "If you do just ring; I will get here as quick as I can." Tom stopped and looked at Cliff who was in visible pain. "You will be sore for a while longer, just take it easy; let your body repair itself. Do you want the curtains opened; it is a nice sunny day?" Tom looked at Cliff, who nodded his head affirmatively. Then Tom opened the heavy white curtains to let in a blast of light and heat.

It felt good and the sun cheered Cliff up. He thought about Mac and where he was. He knew it was the Colonels men who were responsible. Cliff wondered though, why he was not killed or taken with Mac. This remained a mystery to him, as was the question about how the Colonel found them both in the first place. Soon Cliff began to get drowsy and he fell asleep.

Later that day the County Sheriff came in to see how Cliff was doing, but Cliff was sleeping. Sheriff Dan Treadwell knew that this guy was lucky to be alive. He would get down to the details later, there was plenty of time and as he went out he left word at the desk to have the nurse call him when Cliff was awake and well enough to talk. As he came to his car, the Sheriff got in and looked once again at the accident report as he sat in the front seat of the car. One thing

was strange, there were a lot of tracks, the Truck was burned beyond

any use for evidence and all he had was this one guy who someone

tried to kill. Of note was the many tracks around the scene, but these

were not normal size footprints. They were very large and deep in

the ground. Whoever made these tracks was big, really big and really

heavy! He wondered what on earth could be that big and goes

around unnoticed? He shook his head from side to side in the puzzle

of it all and headed back to the Sheriff's department.

Was he dead, where was he if he wasn't dead? The thoughts

crammed his mind as he struggled to open his eyes. Vague memories

of a life past haunted his sleep, if you could call it that. The inability

to wake up, knowing you're asleep, dead, or somewhere in-between.

Yes, this must be hell, a place where the soul doesn't exist, yet it

does exist. In a place that has no time, no sun, no moon, nothing.

That moment in your life when you cannot control a thing, yes this is

hell. But you realize you are still in your body. It is there, at least

you believe it is and yet you cannot touch it. You cannot move;

however you seem to be able to think; but even that is restricted to

what you know. I know nothing, the thoughts raced through his head. If I knew anything, then I would know where I was, and what was happening to me. Suspended, yes that is it. He struggled to maintain the thoughts as the mist clouded his mind. He was suspended in time, in moments between what was and what is now. If there is a God, where is he? Can I find him? Will he listen to me? Suddenly, a sharp prick made him jump and He moved his eyelids slightly.

"You see he is coming out of it" a female voice said.

"Can you bring him out of it quicker" a deep voice asked with authority.

"Yes, I will give him some adrenaline" she replied.

Mac lay there trying to move his eyelids, but they were too heavy; his efforts to make sense of anything were useless. "I know those voices, but who are they? Think Mac" he told himself. Suddenly a thought came to him which seemed to warn Mac about danger that surrounded one of the voices.

Finally, as Mac struggled, one eyelid opened and he saw a room. Nothing registered, he was not on the Ranch, or at the Rev's, or at Cliffs! Wait a minute he thought, a crash. Slowly it came back. He saw Cliff driving, then heard the gunshots, and saw Cliff fall against the steering wheel. Then it all went into a spin. A horrible blackness came over him and sorrow filled him. "Cliff my friend"; Mac muttered his name softly, and then said, "Where are you?"

"Oh, I see your awake now, go ahead and open the other eyelid and look around Mac", a female voice spoke gently

As he opened his eyes he recognized Dorothy a nurse in the hospital ward of Alpha base. She and he had a fling many years ago. "Uh, hi Dorothy; my but you're looking good" Mac smiled weakly

"You are a mess, what did you get into now. You know I told you to be careful; but oh no your cowboy attitude and get it done bravado just about killed you this time. If the Colonel had not of ordered them to keep you alive, you would be dead now!" Dorothy reached over and squeezed him gently, "You know I still love you… you old bag of bones!"

"I know Dorothy but I am too busy for anything too hot, and Dorothy your too hot for me ole gal" Mac chuckled at the thought and it made pain shoot up, he winced and quieted down

"Be careful you have some healing to do." Dorothy stopped as another person entered in

"Dorothy leave us alone, close the door; I don't want to be disturbed" with that the Colonel stopped talking and waited for Dorothy to leave, watching her as she closed the door. Before she left, her eyes gave away the fear in her eyes. They were warning Mac of who just arrived!

"Well I see you are finally awake." Said the Colonel, who smiled at Mac and then mockingly quipped; "I thought we may have to give you honors, a flag, and a 21-gun salute!"

Mac saw the Hitler-esc figure standing firm and tall in his mediocre 5ft ten-inch frame. He with strained himself and said a friendly "Hello Colonel how is murder incorporated"!

"Hey Mac, that is your handle remember; we are just scientists improving humanities lot" The Colonel streamed off until he was quiet

"Yea sure, like the job you did in Montana and to that couple, not to mention all the others you have murdered using those stone age hit men you and your crony genetics people created." Mac was getting angry and he was in no position to peeve him off, so he struggled to smile.

"None of that would have been done if you had kept your place. You know we can't let anyone leave. Not even you; as good as you were. The cardinal rule is there is no leaving the organization. The blood is on your hands, if you had stayed; all of them would have lived. As for the hit men, all we did was help in the DNA and genetics level to improve their live ability on this planet with humans. You see the human genome is much more destructive than these Mortiphilim, the younger improved version of the Nephilim, although we still have some of them roaming around." He smiled at Mac and then said "I did miss you, whether you know it or not. I liked you and gave you favor my friend; why do you think you're still alive?"

"Alive, did you say they would still be alive; that is right up until the time you and your cronies blow everything in the country to kingdom come and then send all your hordes of murderers on America! You have a dark side Colonel, borderline psychotic and Satanic. I was never in that arena; I did all I did for the nation, out of love for America and being Patriotic. I fought with all my ability. That is until I really found out the dark side of this mess you and your people lead here." Mac finished and looked at the Colonel who was now getting mad, he had done it now. Mac thought he should have just kept quiet but that was not his strong suit. It was too late now! Well he would wait for the opportunity to get out of here; he did it once, he will do it again!

"Mac, you left and we know why! Your agent from the group you really work for was caught red handed. That agent talked after some time in our interrogation room on level 13. You left because you knew your cover was blown, not because of your so called Patriotic principles." And Mac…. the Colonel trailed off, rubbed his chin, and then added "You will also be taken to that same area. When I finish with you, well, you will wish we had killed you." The Colonel smiled and laughed a wicked cackle; then added "By the way we left your buddy Cliff. He is probably dead by now; he was nearly that way when my men got there. This is one more whose blood you are responsible for. I will leave you ole boy to heal up a bit before we torture the hell out of you!" laughing again, he said "The Master will be by to see you"! With that the Colonel left abruptly without looking back.

Mac watched him go and said, "You mean Master Lucifer, your delusionary friend and leader who is as crazy as you are?"

Mac was exhausted, but despite what the Colonel said about Cliff being dead; he knew Cliff and being dead does not happen to Cliff. He is a survivor and has an innate ability to live through anything. Mac knew he was alive. He thought on the words of the Colonel and his plans, and then sleep took over. He was in simply too much pain and hurt to go anywhere; let alone fight his way out. If Mac could though, he knew he would have killed the Colonel the moment he came into his room.

Mac awoke to a sound, it was a night nurse adjusting some tubes in his arm and giving him a fresh packet of something. He looked at her in the light of the hospital room. She saw him and smiled "You need more of this to fight infection". She then went out of the room, Mac watching her as she left.

In the corner of the room a shadow had appeared and it suddenly took shape. Out walked a man, but not any man. He was dressed in a sharp business suit, tie, and was polished up and down. But this was no ordinary man. As he came up he greeted Mac.

"Hello Mac, I am glad your back with us", the voice stopped

"Well, if it isn't the Master, pardon me if I don't bow" Mac said rudely then added "I don't like you at all!"

"Well you should, I can do you much good. I can make you filthy rich" with that Lucifer opened up his arms and between his hands he let fly money, gold, change of all kinds appearing out of nowhere, going from one hand to the other; forming an endless stream of riches. Lucifer smiled and then laughed out loud, very loud "Just like that, you see I will arise and yes you will bow to me or die. It has been written of me in Revelation chapter 13 and many other places in the Christians bible. I will rule the nations and they will worship me. I will arise, I will ascend, and I will be like the Most High God." Lucifer stopped and looked at Mac.

"Neat trick, cancel my promotion ole boy; I don't want any part of you" Mac stopped and saw him getting angry.

"You know I can make your life the best on earth, or" Lucifer again stopped and smiled looking at Mac.

"Or you can make my life an unbearable nightmare, yes; I already know that part of your bag of tricks" Mac stopped.

"Think it over Mac, especially when my servants are working on you in the interrogation room, believe me, changing sides to join me will look very tempting to you, just think Mac I will give you unlimited wealth, fame, riches, women, or whatever you want. All you have to do is to submit to me as your lord and master. I have the authority to give you it all Mac, absolutely all of it and I will do that; you will rule as my right hand, people will bow to you and serve you."

Lucifer stopped, turned to go, and then added "Mac you need to be sure to consider this carefully, I could have killed you at any time, but I want you. If I can't have you then no one will. You have shed much blood on my behalf and for that I am grateful"

"Grateful, you; oh, I bet that is truth, gag, gag "Mac gesturing with his finger in his throat, then laughing, as he watched Lucifer; who turned one last time and said "I will have the last laugh on you Donovan Mac Eoghain. I have known you from birth, it was I who named you in your native Celtic tongue the "strong fighter" and that is what you are. But it is I who has been with you. I have watched you from birth and you were destined to help me in this hour. If you deny your destiny, then I will deny your life. I will kill you and you will go the Sheol, the place of the dead; where my angels would love to get their hands on you."

Mac shuddered, he told no one his real name, and yes it was Donovan Mac Eoghain. He was Irish but with strong Celtic roots. He had been named after a "Brown Haired Chieftain" in his clan. But now as he was alone, the words haunted him. He knew he had gone too far, said too much. Now in the quietness of the early morning, he was alone; as alone as he had ever been. How he wished for the caress of Melissa, his love that was killed by the Colonels men. No, he would get the last laugh, but he needed time to mend and a friend somewhere in here to help him escape.

Cliff moved a bit and stood up beside the bed. They had taken out the tubes, removed the Catheter, and he had been walking the hallways for a couple of days. He was sore but he was much improved. His ribs were still wrapped and pained him some; but he could move. The shoulder also ached and he had been working it slowly to get it to move normally. The Doc had told him they would release him soon, but he would need time for everything to heal and return to normal. He looked out the large window facing south and saw the community before him. A nice little community he thought. He was not sure of the scene of the accident but it was a couple of hours from the Rev's at least. He was now in Rawlins and he needed a way to get home, not to mention he did not have a ride yet. He had met with the Sheriff and told him that he and Mac were coming from a livestock sale in Wheatland and wanted to go down to Salt Lake

City to buy some equipment for the Ranch. The Sheriff was troubled about the accident and Cliff knew he would not let it alone. But for now, Cliff was free to go home and he knew Cliff's address. Cliff looked his stuff over that was gathered on the table to the side of the bed. He had everything, his keys, wallet, change, and even his cell phone. He grabbed the cell and turned it on. Cliff could not believe it was still working and the battery was not dead. He had Tiger's cell in his phone address book, which he brought up and then pushed Tiger's call mobile number. The phone rang but went into the answering mode; then Cliff spoke quickly "Tiger this is Cliff; Mac and I have been in a bad accident, can't talk now but call me ASAP, I am in a hospital in Rawlins, will give you details later" with that the call ended. Cliff sought for a cord to charge his phone and one of the aides went and got an extra one that would fit his.

Gin and Tiger had been in the high country and now they had been coming down the mountain. It was a good hour and a half to get from the campground high in the Big Horns to the interstate that ran the valley between Casper and Billings. They would head to the interstate, and then proceed to Gin's house. From there plans were to go back to the Rev's. It had been a good time and now as Gin drove, Tiger was looking out at the passing mountains. Cold clear streams filled with brook trout flowed like a ribbon in the valleys. This was beautiful country and he would remember the campground, it was where he truly came to know Yeshua, his Messiach.

"Gin, it is sure beautiful here" Tiger spoke gently as he watched the scenery

"I know, I just love this place" Gin replied

As they drove the traffic was heavier than usual. The road they were traveling served as a cutoff between the western and eastern portion of the state. Many people took the route over the mountains, as it was quicker than going around. They finally reached the bottom and went through the small western town near the interstate. The decision was made to continue driving and eat later on so they headed south on the interstate towards Kaycee. As Gin drove, Tiger grabbed his cell phone and saw that he had a message. He had not looked at his phone in a week or more. But now, it clearly had a message. He called to retrieve the message and heard Cliff speaking on the other end of it. He put up the phone and worry showed on his face. He looked at Gin and she saw the look on his face.

"What is the matter, who was that on the phone?" asked Gin

"It was Cliff, seems he and Mac had been in an accident. He said he was in a hospital in Rawlins, but he did not say a thing about Mac ". Tiger finished and looked puzzled wondering what had happened. "There is only one hospital there, so we can go get him and Mac if they are there; but first let's stop by the house and drop all this stuff off. We will call the Rev and let him know.

In a few hours Gin had both herself and Tiger at the house. They ate a quick bite of lunch and dropped off all the camping gear. Then she took the large Suburban and left her car. They filled up with gas and treats, and headed out towards the hospital.

Cliff was on the bed and half asleep when the phone rang. He picked it up and was glad to hear Tiger on the other end. "Cliff, Gin and I are now heading to get you; we have the Suburban and it has plenty of room. Are you alright? What happened? You did not say where Mac was. I will put you on speaker phone, so go ahead Cliff; we will listen as we travel." Tiger stopped and was very anxious to hear the details

"Well Tiger I cannot tell you much details over the phone, but I will later. I am banged up pretty bad. It seems that when we left the Rev's somewhere along our route, we were ambushed. I got shot;

Macs truck went out of control and when it flipped over I passed out. I awoke in this hospital bruised, beaten, and somewhat bloodied; but I am okay. I can move. I cannot say more, there are ears listening; if you catch my drift. Just be here, I am on the second-floor room 242. The doctor said I could leave, so it is good timing." Cliff paused

"Cliff, we will get there as soon as we can. We are glad you are okay. I know my uncle, he is a survivor. No matter where he is at, he will get in touch with us as soon as he can, but I know that this Colonel probably has something to do with it" Tiger stopped and heard Cliff again

"You said it not me, I will see you guys soon and be careful; keep your eyes open if you know what I mean" Cliff looked out the window and then towards the door of the room and the nurse was coming; then he said, "I have got to go Tiger, just be here"

With that the phone went dead, and Tiger hung up and said to Gin "What do you think?"

"Well it doesn't sound good and I know that we must be careful. This Colonel is up to something no good and we must be on guard for anyone following us." Gin stopped and turned to see Tiger looking at her. She could see the concern on his face. Tiger turned away and thought about it. This was bad news, and the worse is, he

did not know where his uncle was; but he knew that the Colonel was

behind it.

Chapter Eight: Expunged

By mercy and truth iniquity is purged: and by the fear of the LORD

men depart from evil Proverbs 16:6.

The day was bright and sunny with blue sky as far as the eye

could see. Just the kind of weather most folks in these parts love so much. The far ranges of the Teton's could be seen in the distance with just a hint of snow on the top. Around them was a green mountain meadow and as the Rev sat there, he looked at the Prophet who was speaking.

"You see Rev; you need to be on the watch for these people. They are a rough evil bunch and they have it in mind to kill Christians. It is not that they are picky in their choice in going after Christians. But many believers are patriots and as such they are potential enemies and thus targeted. No doubt these guys will kill just about anyone in their way." The Prophet finished and took a drink of Ice tea and ate a bite of cold fried chicken that was provided for the meeting. The Prophet and Benjamin his aide had left early to meet with the Rev. They were aware of the latest troubles being brought to bear by the Colonels men. The Prophet had dealt with them before. The Prophet knew the source of the Colonel's inspiration, it was dark and very troubling; yet the Prophet knew that these things would occur in the last days. The dark one will appear as prophesied and many would accept him. All things were being made ready for that advent of end time appearances.

"I know Prophet, and thanks for the information on the Nephilim or whatever they call this new breed. I got a call from Gin, one of our people who said that Mac and Cliff had an accident. They were on their way to get Cliff after he had called Tiger, Mac's nephew. Mac though is missing and it is believed the Colonel has him. They will pick Cliff up and come to the Ranch." The Rev stopped, and turned around to see the others who came with them casually talking and enjoying the scenery.

"Well, I can tell you that Mac is a great asset, and as of yet he has a decision to be made as to whom he will follow in all this. But I am confident and have faith; Mac will come to know the Lord. But he is the kind of guy that you need to keep the Colonel at bay. The Prophet finished speaking, and suddenly was prompted by the Spirit in him.

"Rev, we must be going; I have some things to take care of right now." The Prophet motioned to his aide and they walked to the car as the Rev walked alongside.

"Will we see you again soon Prophet?" the Rev asked, knowing that not many people were able to see him, let alone speak to him!

"I am sure sometime in the future, but as you know; I do my work behind the scenes and occasionally am in the midst of it. Yet there is much to do here and be concerned with. Remember what I told you Rev and be sure to fast and pray; as if I need to remind you". The Prophet stopped and smiled, then he grabbed the Rev and gave him a hug with a blessing, praying; "Shalom, until we meet again"

The Rev watched as the Prophet drove away. The meeting had been very sudden and he had to leave without notice and meet with him concerning some things coming. The Prophet told him that betrayal had found its way into the group. The Prophet further said that the group's identity and location were revealed and the enemy had found a way into the group. However, this infiltration would involve someone whom the Rev knew and loved. Deceit and double-cross was what the Colonel was about and through this method the Prophet warned that the Colonel had set already in motion a plan to kill everyone at the Ranch, including the Rev and his family. The Prophet told them to move out of the Ranch to another secure location, but also said that very soon all of it would be out in the open. As the Rev stood there he thought deeply to himself "how could this occur at our group, we had always warned about it; but now it has happened! Who or what was responsible?" the Rev

wracked his brain as the thought of a traitor had made their way into

the group. As he did, a horrible thought came to him, then just as

quickly the Rev thought "no, it couldn't be"! He would wait for the

betrayer to come clean and then deal with it then. The Rev looked

around and saw those with him and said "Come, we must be going."

As the afternoon sun burned down upon the highway, the small

group left with the Rev driving and his group speaking excitedly

about everything that day. Yet the Rev told none of them what he

had been told according to the Prophets warning on the matter. He

said, "otherwise the betrayer might feel threatened and do something

worse". As they drove the Rev wondered about the mysterious

Prophet, even to him, he was an enigma. The Prophet did not make

phone calls; get on the internet, or do what many people today do.

He does one thing, which is, be a Prophet. If you are to be told

something, it is in person with the Prophet. But not even the Rev

knew how the Prophet was able to appear and re-appear seemingly

everywhere at times. But no doubt, this was a real life Jewish

Prophet who believed in the Messiach Yeshua. The Rev was glad to

have him on his side, and the Rev trusted this Prophet. Unlike other so-called Prophets, when this one prophesied; it came to pass. The anointing he had, well it was unlike anything the Rev had ever seen. Miracles were common place for this Prophet and the supernatural was where he operated.

Yet it still nagged at the Rev having a threat inside the group. Why would they betray Mac who was helping them? No matter the reason, the stakes now were very high, and the cost will be blood if they were not careful. Enemies within and enemies without; the Rev thought to himself "your enemies will be those of your own household" and again he pondered "think not I am come to bring peace". No doubt these are the days that can cause sorrow of soul and anguish of spirit for many. The only peace and hope anyone will have is in Yeshua Ha Massiach, Jesus Christ! The Rev adjusted his posture and his grip on the steering wheel as he thought on these things. Then he settled in for the long drive.

"There he is said Gin as she looked at Tiger who was now driving! I am glad he could reach us before we got here so we could pick him up. Out front was Cliff in a wheelchair with a hospital aide who had pushed him to the edge of the pickup area for patients. He could have waited inside but the day was beautiful and they enjoyed small talk and the sun as Cliff had waited for his ride. Now with his ride here, Cliff smiled and was glad to see people he recognized.

"Hey Cliff, man you look good, a sight for sore eyes; I missed you" Said Tiger as he ran to Cliff and started to push him to the suburban.

Gin came close and gave Cliff a hug very gingerly and asked, "how are you doing, really?"

"Fine Gin, I am glad to see you and Tiger! Plus, I am really glad to be getting out of here" Cliff said as he anxiously waited to be able to get in the vehicle and out of here, the sooner the better. He looked around to see if anyone was watching, of course in this small town many eyes would be watching I suppose, Cliff thought to himself. But he did not see anything out of the ordinary, so he felt better. Tiger opened the door to the back seat of the suburban and he helped Cliff up who needed just a little extra effort to climb into the seat. He felt some pain as he did so and grimaced, then gritted his teeth and smiled saying "that hurts"

"Be careful you two" Gin admonished watching Tiger help Cliff

"I am" Said Tiger and then shut the door as Cliff adjusted himself in the seat

Tiger got in and the three of the headed out of town and hit I 80 heading east. Tiger had filled up as he and Gin got into town. They also picked up more snacks and drinks. As they left the last of the town, the rolling southern plains were all around them. Herds of Antelope ran as they drove by. Scrub sage dotted the landscape as the long road lay head. By now the semi-truck traffic was filling the roadway along with other cars and as they drove they were surrounded by vehicles. Tiger moved to the left lane and passed a semi. Then he moved into the right lane again. But he had an uncomfortable feeling inside. He had little experience in this kind of stuff. He did investigate, report, and in this case, had found a way to hack the computer at Alpha, but he did not realize the mess he would get into for doing this. Now though, it was life or death and Mac was still missing. He looked at Gin and she was dozing off as was Cliff. Tiger looked into the mirror and saw the line of vehicles behind him strung out for miles. He thought to himself "How could anyone live in this desolate place, but one thing is for sure; he was glad to be here with Gin. Yes, indeed; Gin was alright and he would stick close to keep her safe."

But what the three did not notice was that one of the semis behind them had been following their vehicle from the edge of Rawlins and now was some three trucks back, lost in the myriad of vehicles traveling I 80. It was a long wide road on an endless sea of plains grasses and sage, where could a vehicle disappear to? Nowhere and that was why on this road it was easy to follow someone. From a distance, two pairs of eyes watched the suburban ahead of them. Those inside knew full well they could follow them with little trouble of being detected.

Mac twisted his face in pain as the pressure was put on the tight bands. Straight out of the Kings dungeons in Europe this torture device had arrived. It was called a 'rack' and was the cause of many a poor prisoner's agony and death. Once hooked up, there was little chance of escape. The Colonel apparently could not wait for Mac to be healed so here he was on level 13, brought here at 3 am in the morning. He had been given no notice, nor had he been given anything to eat or drink in some time. His arms and legs both were each bound by a long rope with a leather strap around the ankles and wrists. The rope was then tied to end of a long drum from which spindles on each side of the drum were used to wind the rope up. As the spindles were turned, the cylinder would wind the rope and then click in place. This thing was antique, but the Colonel had gotten it somewhere and it still worked good, much too good for Mac. His back was on some rollers and provided a very uncomfortable place to lie down. They had been stretching him like this since he arrived down here and as they tightened it again, Mac could feel his joints. They seemed to be coming out of the sockets. The attendant left him and he lay there as the stench of the place entered his nostrils. The pain was searing and in his mind, he knew this kind of torture. He had undergone this in training years ago. Then there was the time he had been captured by Chinese agents who wanted information as to why he and his men were seen in Hong Kong. That was tough and Mac nearly died that time. But he escaped by a hairs breadth. Now here he was in a portion of Alpha base where few escape. Except for Mac that is, he had gone out this way before. He knew how to get out, but he needed to have an opportunity.

"Well hello there, having a bit of a rest are we Mac" mocked the Colonel as he smiled contentedly

"You are the only one I know who really gets turned on by causing someone pain" Mac tried to look up but he was unable. He gritted his teeth as pain flowed through his body and then he realized he could not feel his hands or feet.

Then swiftly the Colonel picked up a flat oak board and hit the bare feet of Mac with a loud thump. He looked up as Mac yelled in pain. "There, that is more like it. I want pain, I want you to suffer, and by the way Mac, that hurt. I love it! I will break you or kill you and frankly today I don't care which."

The Colonel then hit the other foot harder and this caused Mac to nearly faint, the pain now in his feet were intolerable but inside his mind as the pain tore away at the fabric of his soul, he knew he would not give in. But God help them if he manages to get out of this because as he lay there he will kill those devils or die trying.

The Colonel strode over to Mac's side and saw his eyes were closed. He slapped Mac on the face, and there was no response. He slapped him again and slowly Mac opened his eyes. As the Colonel looked at him, he saw the contempt and blood red hatred for him.

"Ah, yes, just what I like. Now I can really give you pain. When you hate me like that, adrenalin pours throughout your body and you can endure more. I can really have fun now. I could kill you with no trouble at all. I could pull you apart like they did in the inquisition.

Man do I love to read how those priests conducted the horrid tortures on those innocent people. I just love it. But if I killed you now, I would have no more fun. No, we will extend this for as long as we can, yes that is what we will do. You will pray for me to kill you Mac. Yes, you will pray that I will kill you quickly. Oh, by the way how do you like my little piece of 12th century equipment here, it was a special donation on my part to the cause of which I serve. The cause of pain and destruction, just call me the 'Destroyer'." The Colonel then nodded to the attendant who then went to the spindle wheel and started to turn it.

Mac felt the pressure and soon he heard a pop, his shoulder went into extreme pain and he knew it was separated. The other one was still intact, but soon it began to give way; then the pressure was let up. Immediate relief poured into his body, although it was beyond aching. The pain beyond anything you could describe, yet Mac lay there with revenge in his heart and blood red eyes of a killer. He would get back, God help them now, but I will get revenge!

They unstrapped Mac and now had to carry him. His shoulder was out of joint and he could not walk for the pain in his feet from the board the Colonel used on him. They threw him in a dark cell, and closed the door. Mac lay there in the darkness alone. He hurt, couldn't move, and couldn't walk. His shoulder was separated and now he couldn't even use his arm. Plus the other one was so sore, it could barely move.

Outside the door he heard the Colonel speaking to someone. "There that will ensure this guy will go nowhere. He can't walk, leastwise fast enough to get out without us knowing it. He can't use his arms, and he is really messed up, I would say good job people"

Soon it was quiet and as Mac lay there he tried to focus. A friend, he needed a friend. No matter what happens he would not cave in. He would die rather than give into the Colonel who by now was showing his true color. But Mac knew he would get through this somehow, from deep inside he felt hope. No matter how bad it was, there would be a way to get out of this. Hope suddenly had replaced his rage. The rage and hatred was from his past and the cold blood killer instinct which had made him the best of them all. He had been murder incorporated, but now, all he wanted was peace and as he lay there in pain, Hope was much better than rage or hate. Soon Mac fell asleep and all around him was darkness.

Gin's phone rang and she picked it up, looking at the interstate that lay before her. She recognized the area and knew they were about an hour away from the Ranch. "Hello" Gin said as the alarmed voice of the Rev said "I have been on the phone with Squire Dickens. Two more of the Remnant groups have been hit. These were not on our dummy list that the Colonel got. It looks like another inside leak, maybe the same person. One was hit in Savannah and another one in Philly. It is not known how many escaped, but Squire Dickens said he had calls from members of each group. They all said it was a night assault and many were dead." The Rev stopped and Gin responded quickly "Again, they hit again? How can they get away with this? Doesn't anyone see what is happening? Where are the Police?" Gin sounded frustrated.

"I know Gin, but understand that the people around the area only see official Government vans with Police. They think it is a legit raid on a drug house or a gang. But whatever the public may think, they don't think for a moment that innocent people are being killed. It is all undercover. Over the years we have watched this unfold again and again. They give false media reports and usually lay this to drugs or terrorism. Besides many Americans are asleep and truly believe that this is America and things like that don't happen here"

The Rev quieted down and then said "Look Gin you guys are not to come here; can you go somewhere else? I mean where others can gather. I had also spoken to another source of mine and he said that we have an inside leak in our group. I believe our Ranch is on the list and they will hit soon."

Gin thought as the phone quieted down and said, "Let me think Rev, where we can put you all!" Then a voice behind Gin asked "What is happening?" It was Cliff and he overheard some of the conversation. "If you need a place, you can come to my Ranch; I have plenty of room and many friends who have helped us and Mac before"! Cliff stopped and waited for an answer

"Look Rev, Cliff says we can go to his place and he has room for everyone." Gin stopped, waited, and then agreeing spoke quickly "Okay Rev, I will give you to Cliff, he will tell you directions to his place." As Cliff gave the Rev directions to the Ranch, Tiger was listening intently but now he saw a semi that had been following behind for two hours. It never varied or tried to pass any other trucks. It stayed put. Well he would keep an eye on it.

Meanwhile, Cliff finished speaking to the Rev and gave the phone back to Gin, as he fell back into his seat and closed his eyes. He was exhausted and ached all over. Cliff opened one eye and saw Gin on the phone.

"Thanks Gin" said the Rev who then motioned to his wife who was making dinner for them. The Rev was standing in the kitchen area and said to his wife as Gin listened "I want you to take the women and kids, a few men with you to Cliffs, I will meet you later. I must stay here gather papers and destroy some information so the Colonel won't get it. I will also have some of the brethren who are vets stay with me. We will be along later; but you must be gone in a couple of hours." The Rev then turned to Gin on the phone and asked "Did you hear that? It will take some time, but expect them in the early morning hours and Gin you guys must be prepared for anything!" "Got it Rev, we will look for Cynthia and the rest in the early morning hours, we can make it to Cliffs in a couple of hours or so from where we are at." With that Gin hung up the phone and told Tiger to turn off at Laramie and head north from there to Cliff's Ranch.

The drive to the turn off at Laramie was some twenty minutes away and now Tiger neared the town. He came to the exit and headed into Laramie. After making it through Laramie he would head north out of town and take the cutoff to I 25. From there it would be open sailing so to speak. Tiger left the town heading north. In a short time, he had driven a couple of miles and they were close to the cutoff coming up. As he drove, the mirror reflected a familiar semi a half a mile back and Tiger did a double take of it. It was still following them.

"Hey guys, we are being followed" Tiger said motioning with his finger behind him.

"You sure Tiger" said Gin and Cliff together as they looked behind and saw a plain looking semi in the distance. Then Gin looked at Tiger and asked, "You sure, I mean it could be anybody"

"No way, I have been watching these guys for a couple of hours and now since they are still behind us, I am positive they are following us." Tiger finished and was followed by Cliff's voice which confirmed Tigers suspicions "Yes I saw that same semi in Rawlins. They drove by the hospital as I was waiting for you guys. They both stared at me as they went by. Yep they are following alright we have to lose them."

As they drove Cliff spoke up "You know I have some friends close by here. Let me call them, they can pick up on this truck." With that Cliff took out his phone and quickly dialed, waited for a moment. An inaudible sound could be heard on Cliff's phone as he said "Hey can you help me out. I am with some friends and am heading home. There is this semi following us for several hours now. We have turned off again and again." Cliff waited and he listened and then answered "Yes, it still follows us from some distance." Cliff finished and again listened then said, "We are some thirty minutes from your turn off." Cliff stopped, and then quickly spoke "We will bypass you. We are in a blue suburban with Wyoming plates, there are three of us and I am in the back, which you will be able to see me clearly." Cliff smiled as he looked at Gin in the front and then said; "Good, how long can you stall them?" There was a pause and Cliff listened intently; "Well that will work thanks and by the way, we may need you and some of the guys at the Ranch soon, very soon." Cliff hung up and then explained to Tiger and Gin who had been listening. "We are not too far from the turnoff, I will show you when we get close.

When we pass by, they will take it from there. But we must hurry and get out of sight. They can hold them for some time, but they will have to let them go. If it is a government project, then they may have more trouble with them, but they will stop them no matter what!"

As they came close to the turn off Cliff motioned to Tiger and Gin. As they passed by, they saw two police cars and three black Humvees. They waved at Cliff as he motioned to them. The Semi was nowhere to be seen. They found a road which they took to a scenic overlook behind some large trees which hid the parking lot. The three got out and followed a path to the viewing area where you could see the valley below with a stream that ran alongside the road. Gin had taken out some binoculars she had under the seat. "These were my dad's, we kept them after he passed, I knew they would come in handy" Gin surveyed the area below and shouted "You didn't tell me your friends were Patrolmen."

Cliff was watching the area and could see they had the semi stopped. He then spoke answering Gin; "Well one of them is, or at least was! The entire group is made up of former Vets and was in the same black ops projects Mac and I was in. They are a specialty force, you could say. Gin could see two men out of the semi who had what looked like papers out. The police cars looked official and the men looked like Patrolmen. The Humvees were both in front of and behind the semi, and armed men in black gear stood watching. Cliff could see the lights and knew what they were doing. He spoke up "They will thoroughly inspect their truck and trailer. Then will also write them a ticket if need be; doing all they can to keep them waylaid until we lose them." Cliff laughed as he watched but then turned serious as he said, "If these guys are pushed or threatened, they will kill them straight way!"

"Let's go and get out of here, I don't want to see that semi again or those guys in it." Tiger said walking to the suburban.

As they made their getaway, the semi was stopped cold. Now a long drawn out process of questions, and possible violations along with an inspection made it impossible for the men in the semi to follow Tiger, Gin, and Cliff anymore, who by now was nearing the end of the canyon. As relief finally settled in the group drove out of the canyon and on to I 25 leaving the cutoff and the semi far behind. They would be home soon; it would not be long now to Cliffs Ranch. The Ranch itself was far enough away from Macs place it would not be connected to him. Cliffs place was a real cattle ranch, which would provide good cover so that no one would suspect anything else. They should be safe from the Colonel there.

The fire had been burning for some time and now the last of the papers to be destroyed were in the fire. The Rev had sent two men with important Remnant documents to another group in Idaho. He also told them their new location at Cliffs Ranch. They would not be informed as to why the Rev's groups moved or the trouble of an inside leak, he would take care of that later. For now, though, these documents must be safe and far away from this place. The Rev would also have copies of the stuff and would destroy it if need be. They would now be charged with the safe keeping of the information that if it somehow found its way into the wrong hands could literally mean death for many. They had senators, congressmen, policemen, sheriffs, and professionals of all kinds in the Remnant groups. All private and fiercely dedicated to keep America with its constitution intact, even to the point of death. There were many who had no idea just how popular the ideal of American patriotism and the constitution was. Not even those who were trying to destroy

America had any clue as to the number that swelled the ranks of the Remnant.

The Rev looked around as one of the men came close that had been watching the area. As he came near to the Rev, he bent down and whispered in his ear "they are now getting close. We spotted them not too far away, it won't be long now. Are you about ready?" He asked

"Yes, I am, where are the others" said the Rev grabbing his briefcase.

"Getting ready for war, even here, at this time, at this place; we are ready Rev" he stopped and looked at the Rev, with a very serious look, he was ready to fight and die.

"I know they are coming and that we may not make it out, but know this, it is not over; there are others who back us, we will win"

Smiling the Rev patted him on the back and said, "let's go." As they both went out the door and neared the vehicles, the other men came running and yelling "they are here". With that bullets flew towards them from several directions.

The Rev heard a bullet fly by his head as a "Zing" was clearly heard and then the sound of "thunk", as it made its way into the car the

Rev was now behind. The Rev had a 45 and a few clips, his extra ammo was in the trunk but there was no way to get it. He looked out and a bullet hit the windshield above him. His men were firing and he saw one of the brethren get hit that was by the house. He fell to the ground and lay motionless. The Rev then saw something standing over him. It was huge and the eyes glared out as it stood there over the dead man. The Rev took careful aim and shot at the huge figure which immediately ducked and ran away. He had missed; somehow this thing had gotten wind of him before he could kill it. Around him he heard another of the men get hit and soon the Rev knew he had to find another place. He got up and ran to the house and flew into the door and as he did screaming pain hit him in the back shoulder and he went down. Blood was flowing, but not too bad as another of his men came crashing into the house through the window.

"Rev I shot two of them several times and they kept coming, what are these creatures?" The man looked out and could see the huge figures regrouping near the barn. Soon another of the brethren came in through the back door.

"I got one of them, shot him in the head and he went down. You got to hit them square in the temple; otherwise it seems these bullets don't do any good." Breathing hard, catching his breath he reloaded and looked out.

The Rev pulled his way to the window and felt the bullet in his muscle. The Rev looked out and saw eight of these huge creatures come walking toward the house. As they did bullets came out of nowhere. The barrage hit the group and they went down, all of them quickly. From somewhere, there were people firing hitting them.

Soon out of the darkness, the Rev saw a group of darkly clad, heavily armed men with laser sights and night vision googles on. They came in as they shouted, "we are friendlies", "don't fire"! In through the door came a man that looked exactly like Mac. The Rev looked at him and said, "glad you made it Mac".

"I am not Mac, I am his twin" nickname is Ace and this is my squad, and yes you don't know a thing about us and we will keep it that way. Mac called us in to watch this place before he left. We really hate the Colonel and more so now that they have Mac."

"Well glad you made it!" The Rev saw the other men helping his wounded. Soon a medic came to the Rev and said, "come over here to the table, I will remove the bullet and stitch it up. I have some meds for the pain. In a few days you will be ready to wrestle a bear Rev." the medic smiled and helped him to the table.

"What were those things, Nephilim?" the Rev asked

"Well sort of, a modern breed of genetics. They look human, dress human, but they are not human, leastwise all the way. Their make-up is such you need to hit them square in the head before they will die. But if you don't, well you will be short work for them. They are bloody killers but tonight they took a bath in their own blood. They did not know we were there as we came downwind from them. We took them by surprise." Ace finished and said, "Call the clean-up crew, we must be out of here quick, and then call it in when we are gone"!

"Aye Sir, will do" a voice replied

Ace looked around and said, "is this all you have?"

"Yes, the rest are dead. I had hoped to get out of here before this place was hit. I was warned and wanted to leave." The Rev spoke as he jerked when the medic began to work on his back

"No need to worry about the bodies of the Nephilim, they always pick up and carry their own away. When these things hit, they seem to appear out of nowhere. They make very deadly hit teams. But in the many years of following these things, we have developed a strategy to kill them." Ace finished and then asked, "You guys need help getting to the next location?"

"No, I will have one of my guys drive, we are late in getting there, but thanks to the Lord sending you; we will be able to make it".

"Good grief, I have never been an answer to anyone's prayer." Ace smiled speaking in a surprised tone.

As the Rev was helped to his vehicle it was now early morning and the sun was casting welcoming warmth to the fields surrounding the area. The Rev saw that all the vehicles were government marked and official looking. "Who are you guys anyway, FBI, CIA, or someone else?" The Rev looked at Ace questioning him

"No not the FBI, we are CIA; that is the Good ones in the CIA. You will never see us again, and if anyone asks you, we don't exist. I am sure you know Mac is being kept by the Colonel; we have followed the whole thing. But, the good news is Mac will escape soon to join you. The plans are in the works, but he is in bad shape. Tell him hi when you see him. He will be puzzled and deny I exist, but that is okay; it is our lot for being born into a family that has generations of experience going back to Lincoln's assassination. We are born to live and work in the shadows Rev, to be the ones hidden that can bring about in this nation what is supposed to be." Ace finished and looked around and then added "we must hurry here guys"!

The Rev looked puzzled at the information he just heard. Generations of experience of working in the shadows going back to the Lincoln assassination! That is interesting but what does it mean? The Rev was helped to the car and saw the clean-up crew arrive. Phony reports would be released and the Rev would never come back here again. As the Rev looked up he saw a familiar figure on a hill towards the east. The sun bathed him in light as he could see it was the Prophet. So that's it, the Prophet; go figure the Rev thought, behind the scenes, here he is; the Prophet. He had a hand in our rescue but I don't know how, except that God does work in mysterious ways! Indeed, he does as he waved at the Prophet.

There was no reply, and as the Rev and his men drove away from the Ranch, he looked once again to see the Prophet and he had vanished.

The Rev and his men finally reached Cliffs. They drove on to the ranch house, as men on the bluff signaled by radio that a car was coming. Tiger and Gin looked out and saw the Rev in the car with his men and raced outside to greet them. Cynthia came out of the house and ran to the Rev, leaving a few of the women on the porch that also had come to see who had arrived. They watched as the Rev got out and as he did Cynthia grabbed him and immediately hugged him. They gave each other a kiss as Cynthia began looking at his wound, soon stopping as she saw it was well taken care of, very professional. It was well bandaged and clean. As Cynthia smiled contently to have the Rev back, he stretched his legs. He reached out with his left hand to grab Gin and Tiger, saying "Glad to see you two how is everyone?"

"We are all fine, what happened?" Gin asked the Rev

"Well the Colonel hit us hard and for a little while we thought we were goners. I mean the men were hitting the guys or creatures who attacked us and it was like it had no effect. We held up in the main ranch house and were making our final stand the three of us as a group of them came at us. Then shots rang out and soon it was over. Mac had called in some help to watch the Ranch. I may have had doubts about him before, but you know Tiger, I trust him now! By the way, I met your uncle Ace, the twin of Mac", the Rev smiled and looked at Tiger.

Tiger looked puzzled and said "Rev, I have no Uncle Ace"

"He said that would be the reply if we told Mac, but it also means that not even you would know of him! For some reason, which I am not privy to; Ace is a mystery" the Rev finished and smiled

"It was close but tonight I saw the Lord deliver us out of pure evil and I am glad. Tonight, I will explain what happened and what we may do next, but rest assured I will enjoy all your company tonight. To be with friends is a good thing." With that, they went inside the house.

On the porch were some of the brethren and on the edge of the porch Sun and Ray, Cliff's two Aussie shepherds who lay quietly, contented that their owner had finally gotten home. The group sat around chatting and knew full well the toll that had been taken, of those whose lives were lost this past month. They were shot up, many killed, and other remnant groups had been taken down. They knew that it was headed for a full-scale takedown of America by these unseen forces and they now were not alone in that struggle to keep both God and country, constitution and republic safely intact.

Chapter Nine: Triumph

Lo, this is the man that made not God his strength; but trusted in the abundance of his riches, and strengthened himself in his wickedness

Psalm 52:7

Deep under the Pentagon a meeting has been going on. A group of people are at a long table, water glasses are scattered, as are drinks, and the bar is open. There are about twenty high ranking officials in all avenues of government work. Among those at the table sitting alongside these people were Pleiadean's; Elanah and Londo. These two are paramount to the plans of those bringing in Project Black Light. As the meeting gets underway, Four Star General Edward Myers stands up, looking around the room, then he speaks. He is the director of North American Military Operations or NAMO being the short code name.

"General Carlson has just informed me of recent developments and I have asked him to start the ball rolling on an important issue. General will you stand up and tell us the situation."

"Yes, General Myers I was prepared to do so, but first I want to bring on Colonel Pickett who is our man in the field for Operation Viper. He has just arrived and I wanted him to update us first." With that Lt. General Carlson motioned to Colonel Pickett, who stands up immediately.

Colonel Pickett a tall and muscular build is a career man. He is now the lead officer in the field coordinating Operation Viper directly under General Carlson. He stands up adjusting his stance as he looks around the room, and then proceeds; "Gentlemen it has come to my attention through our people at Alpha base that Donovan 'Eoghain'

McCowen is at the base. He is being tortured by Colonel Schmidt. You know him by his name Mac, or better yet 'death incorporated'."

"Why is that important Colonel?" Asked President Mitchel, who was sitting at one end.

"Because sir, he belongs to the family 'Eoghain' in Celtic, McCowen in English. He is of a very powerful family. Sir you tell them!" Pickett looked at General Carlson who prepared to take the floor, but was interrupted by General Myers.

"Excuse me General Carlson", Gen Myers stands as he sits his drink down. "I want to detail some of what we know of this man. Unless you understand who he is and the background, which I am personally aware of; you may not be fully appreciative of the situation which faces us."

The General stopped and looked around the room as President Mitchel speaks up "Go ahead General I am very interested in what you are about to tell us."

"Gentlemen, Mac as he is known, has connections and His family is known in our work as the "circle" or the "Guardian's". It is very strong and has its own agenda and we want no part with them at this time. They have roots going back to George Washington himself and have put the secrecy in the Secret service they have done for this country. While they are not our friends, they are not our enemies, yet and I do not want them in this over Mac. I don't care how much this Colonel Schmidt hates him", General Edward Myers stopped and looked at both the President and General Carlson; who now were nodding their agreement.

"Colonel Pickett, move ahead with your contact at Alpha base. Make sure that Mac escapes and he has help getting out". General Myers again stopped and sat down. Myers knew Mac and they had dealings going way back, he liked Mac and hoped he was not too late. He knew Schmidt would kill him in a second if he could. The General also knew the very dark morbid side of the Colonel, which liked to play with his prey before he killed them. It gave him some blood thirsty demonic thrill over doing it this way. The General disliked it very much as it went against his training and military ethics. Besides, he did not like this Colonel Schmidt at all.

The President looked around the table of those seated and then said "I know his family, but did not know of this Mac as you call him. But I have known the McCowen family for many years. They have always supported me and donated to my campaign. I had also never heard of this 'Circle or Guardians' either." The President stopped

and waited a moment. This man had made history as the first duly

elected Black President of the United States, whose full name is;

James Carter Mitchel. Mitchel is halfway through his second term as

President. He is a former military veteran, and had worked in black

ops. At Harvard his grades were outstanding. He is a legal scholar

and excelled in the debate team. He has an ability to communicate

and also to bring to the table his ideas. He can handle political

opposition and his debate skills are used extensively. In short, many

of his adversaries are wary before they take him on in any political

issue. His grandparents were children of share croppers that had

been slaves at one time until they managed to escape to the north.

After the Civil war they were freed and were given land and they

worked it. Today he is very wealthy, well respected, and also is in

the midst of the change that he sees is vital for America.

"You would not have seen him sir, he operates completely in secret,

and he is a black ops soldier. He has worked in that capacity for

many years." Colonel Pickett finished and sat down

Today President Mitchel is the proud example of how far America

has come. Except this man is about to make history a second time.

He will formally announce the appearance and contact of aliens on this planet. At a lavish press conference there will be Elanah and Londo; who both speak fluently in many languages and are remarkable. They are almost human like in appearance and are in perfect physical shape. At the President's side, as well, will be Generals Myers. The Cameras will roll, the press and public will be astounded and the many Ufologists will be ecstatic.

"So, both you; Elanah and Londo know that you are to gather and coordinate all the Alien species at the Alpha base in their exodus to our South American underground facilities in the Brazilian rainforest. It is our first natural formation base that utilizes the earth's natural cave systems and surrounding areas for our use. It is code named Zulu Echo One. We want all of you out of the Alpha base in the next month. We will give you coordinates to the new base and they will be expecting you." General Carlson stopped as he eyed the table and swallowed some of his whiskey sour. He then took a puff of his Havana, and sat back in his chair looking at Londo.

"Yes, general we both understand and we will have the others in South America shortly. How long after that are we to meet with the President here to show ourselves to the American public and the world?" Londo finished. He did not like the stuffy room, or the smoke; but he showed no expression. He wanted to move forward in all this. He was disappointed that they have been too slow in coming forth on their end of the deal they had made so long ago.

The President sat up and put his drink down and looked at the rest of those gathered and said "we are putting the final touches on all things. We are targeting within six months' time. When it is all set we will notify you at Zulu base" the President stopped, then looked over to the bar; "give me another scotch will you Charley?"

The bartender nodded and quickly made a drink and ushered it to the President. The night would be long and there would be many things to discuss. But on this night the darkness extended into the oval office and to the very depths of the underground bases where all their devious schemes were being developed. However, these people did not see it as darkness but truth and light. They were bringing in new enlightenment to the world.

What no one outside this meeting could prove was that there are people that have plans in place to take down America. Those seated at this table tonight are part of a huge group of committed individuals that are well organized, well financed, and very dangerous. They are moving many of their bases and people to remote areas out of the country. The date is coming and the aspect of bringing the nation down will also include civil war, and then martial law. The goal is to have a completely renewed system of government and total control by 2020 or sooner if they can. Operation Viper is the sting behind the deception of Project Black Light. The sting of this Viper is so deadly that many working for them today will be found non-gratis; this also includes Colonel Schmidt and Alpha base. The Colonels men had just left Mac. They had beaten him until he went unconscious. His face was bloodied, and both eyes were swollen to the point of being almost closed. Then they gave him a cocktail of psychotropic drugs. These drugs are over the counter therapeutic drugs that many hospitals use, but they are given at toxic levels. They are simply used in the most horrific manner. These drugs are used to affect their central nervous system as well creating horrific visions and dreams, thus prisoners can lose their mind. If they don't lose their mind, they end up dying from the doses or committing suicide. These are tactics that go back to Stalinist Russia. But today many nations use them in secret, like the North Korean regime, and even today's China has this. The ones who live would wind up being shot anyway or put in the ward of the government insane asylum at the mental hospital.

Mac lay there motionless as if dead. As Mac began to look around as he saw horrific visions, creatures that came out of the darkness at him. He tried to fight back, but to no avail. This was useless and had no effect. In a swirling mass of lights, demons, and pain he saw these things whether he opened his eyes or not. He really did not know if he had his eyes open or closed. It was the same mass of hellish creatures. At one point he saw three tall creatures, and like a dragon with short tales behind them. They were standing up and they turned around. They had human faces and spewed out all kinds of filth. They looked at him and prodded him, making fun of him as he lay there. Then they vanished. He could do nothing. His mind began throbbing and his eyes felt as if they would fall out. He began sweating and could find no relief. Then in a few minutes, he started to freeze, his head felt like an ice cube. He tried to roll over but pain hit him from every part of his being and as he grimaced thousands of lights went out in every direction, then he saw a white light, a very bright light which made all other light and visions cease. Mac for a moment felt peace and then heard a voice "Mac, come to me, put aside your ways and seek me. I will give you peace and you will find forgiveness." Mac in this delirium couldn't think for a moment, and then asked, "Who are you Lord"? "I am Alpha and Omega the beginning and the end and everything in between. I am Lord of Lords and King of Kings; I am Jesus Christ, the son of Almighty God and I have appeared to you, so that you will know the real truth. I am the Way, the Truth, and the Life, come my son to me! I will send a messenger to you, hear ye him; he is my prophet"!

Mac stopped breathing for a moment as everything quieted down, did he hear, right? It was the Lord, the same Lord of the bible? He fell back into his delirium. He lay there in between heaven and hell, suspended by chains and looked around. The devil came for a visit and smiled, then laughed doing nothing to free him. Then he saw Melissa, who stood by and laughed, and then she vanished. Everything in a roll, an old-time movie and it played in his mind over and over. He was in the movie and watched himself in the movie. Was he mad? A clear thought, was I mad, I am Mac... No... who am I? The visions and light replayed, then more demonic voices. Mac felt like he was crazy, and pain shot through his body as he moved. He could not take anymore and began screaming. In one last gasp he yelled out "Oh Lord save me" and then he went silent, becoming motionless as a corpse.

Dorothy opened the cell, while the guard watched the hallway for anyone coming. She had been instructed by Colonel Pickett to take care of Mac and get him out. She had the guard who was part of Pickett's team. He and Dorothy among others had been stationed at Alpha base. They answered directly to Colonel Pickett and not Colonel Schmidt. As Dorothy turned on her portable medic light and went in. The place smelled like a sewer and she shone the light to see that Mac was in a heap on the floor. No bed, no bathroom, and not a shred of light. Setting down the lamp, horror griped her as she went to Mac and tried to wake him.

"What have they done to him?" she asked of the guards who now stood behind her.

"They beat him some more and gave him some psycho drugs", one of the soldier's answered and then motioned to one of the other soldiers to bring the medic tray closer.

Dorothy looked over the tray and quickly grabbed a vial and a needle; "Here I will give him this, it will help get that stuff out of him and bring him around. But before we do, come on, let's pop his shoulder in place and see how he is otherwise. This is the best time to do it, as he is passed out!"

Two soldiers held Mac up as Dorothy and another aide grabbed his arm and with a well-placed shove they all heard a pop. Mac jumped, but did not wake up. Dorothy gave him the shot and then grabbed for another vial and then said, "Here I will give him adrenalin shot in the shoulder that will help". After the shots, Dorothy took time to look Mac over and see his condition. They had no equipment here. No x-rays or cat scan available; this would have to do. But there were no bones broken that she could tell. No large lacerations, just many bruises and smaller cuts. She could not clean him up fully as he must look the part. She knew someone would want to see what they were pushing. Mac was not bleeding profusely so she could let it go until they got him to the other room. In her inspection of Mac, she deduced that in spite of his condition, Mac actually fared quite well. He would feel like hell but he would heal. He was lucky to be alive. She was sure the guards that did this when Schmidt had left, intended to kill Mac and do it before the Colonel got back.

"Where is Colonel Schmidt?" Dorothy asked

One soldier spoke up, "Ma'am he has left base for a few days. The General asked to see him so he went as he said to 'see the man'"

"Good, let's get him out of here and into the C.A.C.F. This was the Alien side of level 13, he would be safe; plus, they have a special medic room set up. Mac can recover enough there so that he can get out of Alpha base. I will have Noah make sure no one touches him." Dorothy finished and the soldiers lifted him up, put him on a gurney. It was 3 am in the morning and the shift was to be changed. They went to the main area and the guards were busy talking. They looked over and saw them pushing someone on a gurney with the sheet pulled over.

"Hey, wait a minute, what do you have there?" A sergeant looked at Dorothy

"Well if you must know it is a dead body, we are taking him out of here" Dorothy smiled and then said, "Another one for the compost" The sergeant laughed and said, "well who died?"

"You know the one they call Death incorporated, well he ran into Colonel Schmidt and fulfilled his name. He became death, he died, kaput!" Dorothy finished speaking and they began rolling the gurney away from the main area into the hall.

"Hey, let me see him", with that the sergeant and a few men at the desk ran over.

Dorothy looked at the soldiers with her; who now had their hands close to their autos in their holsters and were getting ready to use them when Dorothy motioned them not to do anything. She grabbed the sheet and laughed "You see this one is not a problem anymore"! "Yea, we heard he was so tough, good riddance to this trash, come on guys let's have a shot of Jack Daniels to celebrate his demise", the men returned to the desk.

Mac had just laid there and Dorothy had held up the covers just enough to hide the fact of Mac's shallow breathing. He was near comatose, and in bad shape; this had saved his life. But as they rounded the corner and headed into the warning area of the Alien section, Mac stirred.

"He is starting to come around, those shots have done the trick, come on let's get him hid. We will get him out this end when the Alien transfer to the South American base begins." Dorothy stopped and went through a check point with two heavily armed men; they also belonged to Colonel Pickett's group. In front of them were double doors with a big red X on it. This was the no-go area for humans.

The aliens on that side never came into the rest of the base and no humans were allowed into that area except for scientists assigned there. There were now in the foyer of the off-limits area and two heavy metal doors which stood locked always were on the west side. Those doors were the sealed off area, kept closed to humans. Two more Guards stood to block any one entering it. These men also were part of Pickett's group. The whole lot of them would leave when the Aliens left. The base was slated to be destroyed and they knew it. Off to the right of where Dorothy and her group came out was a room, which had curtains around it. As they rolled the gurney with Mac on it you could see the area was well lit and soon a hospital room came into view. They had all the equipment needed to work on Mac. As they went in a bed stood ready for Mac, alongside the bed stood a rack with intravenous tubes full of liquid. There were also trays filled with varied nourishment, and monitoring devices. Dorothy looked over to one side of the room and noticed Noah, who immediately saw Mac.

"Noah, this is Mac; you must watch him and keep him safe at all costs. Keep everyone out of the room except for us and our men. Okay" Dorothy looked at Noah

"Noah understands. I like this Mac, he is friend to me. I will protect him." Noah stopped and walked over to the door and stood guard. They took Mac from the gurney and slid him onto the bed. Within a few moments, Mac was being given a sponge bath. Dorothy further cleaned up, and bandaged Mac. They gave him liquid nourishment, direct vitamins through the tube, and then as he needed it, more liquids would be given.

Mac had heard it all, but he was too far gone to say much. He did not care at this point. He had thought he died. It was hell. Then he saw that very bright light!" Mac had never been scared as this. He had never seen those things like he had. Was he in a dream, or maybe even in hell. There was nothing to do but endure it. Whatever happened he did not like it. His own mortality came face to face with him and in the end, Mac had blinked. He was broken, tired, and wanted to die; yet an inner flame burned. It prodded him to believe, there is something better, there is a God, and there is a way out of this. Then he heard a soft voice "Mac believe, just believe", over and over until he fell back into a deep sleep.

"Gin, you and Tiger need to pray right now" The Rev looked serious. "I know Mac is in deep trouble, he needs prayer right now!

Pray for his deliverance out of that place and for his salvation! I have been seeking the Lord about all these things and the Spirit has pointed me to Mac. But it is important right now to pray, there are dark powers trying to snatch his soul before he comes to faith. I believe the Lord has been dealing with him, but know that darkness wants this man.!" The Rev looked around and then with others joining in they prayed for Mac.

Outside Cliff was with his two dogs and the mid-morning sun was shining down on them. The summer has been great, in spite of the Colonel. With all this fuss going on he hadn't been able to do a bit of fishing. Next year he would more than make up for it. He heard the Rev and his people praying for Mac and he admitted to himself that it had him worried about Mac. But if anyone could survive it would be Mac.

Up on the ridge above the Ranch were some of the men on look out. But it was a good day and since their arrival none of the Colonels men even came close. They had sent patrols into town and the semi they described never showed up in the area. There were no suspicious vehicles or new people in town that looked out of place so everyone, as of now, believed it was secure.

As Cliff sat on the porch a car could be seen and the men on the ridge called him on the radio. "Car coming, it has only one driver and no one else following it" the radio went silent and Cliff answered, "Well I will meet them, they will find their way out of here; but be ready!"

A Silver Dodge viper drove into the yard and a man got out. The man saw Cliff and came to him and held out his hand as if to shake it.

"I got the word you had my dad here!" Names Squire Dickens, code name that is, but I am Tom, the Rev's Son

"Well I have heard of you, come on the others are inside. We have some coffee on and a few snacks scattered around." With that Cliff took Tom into house and immediately the Rev saw him and hugged him, both of them stood smiling and joking as people took seats and stood around the room watching.

"Where have you been? How did you know we were here?" The Rev asked Tom

"I was in Idaho and working with others to combine the groups in Idaho Falls. We got the documents and I saw the new location, I wanted to be here and provide assistance if you needed it." Tom stopped and sipped his coffee, "By the way your directions were spot on." He smiled at the Rev and looked around the room."

"Glad you are here Tom, we indeed could use you. We lost some men in the attack, we would have all been killed; but thanks to Mac making arrangements to have some of his people watch the Ranch, we managed to get out alive." The Rev stopped and saw that Tom looked worried and asked, "What is the matter?"

"Well I thought, er, that the Ranch was safe. I did not know you were attacked! I mean you went to so much effort to keep a low profile and not to be found out. How could this happen?" Tom stopped and looked at his Dad

"There was a mole; the Prophet told me that someone would betray us. It was him who told me the danger. I decided to leave right away; we were in the process of leaving the Ranch, when it was hit. We managed to get all the information out to the other groups." The Rev became quiet and noticed that Tom was bothered,

"I am glad you guys made it out, now how about something to eat?" Tom finished and drank some coffee and watched as the others filtered into the kitchen.

"We are going to eat in about 15 minutes" the bell will ring when it is time a voice rang out. It was Cynthia, Tom's mother who by now had already greeted her son and then took to getting food ready to eat.

The Rev walked with Tom and the others into the kitchen as the bell rang some time later. As he did so, he wondered what was bothering Tom. He knew his son, but since he had been in government; he seemed to change somewhat. Then he was a double agent working both sides in order to help the Remnant Group. The Rev wondered if Tom had gotten into something he could not get out of? The Rev Thought about this and then patted his son on the back. Discarding any trouble in his heart with Tom, the Rev knew that everything would work out!

As everyone was gathered to eat, the line formed along the porch and into the kitchen where they picked up their food. But before they began, the Rev prayed and then as he stopped. Tom spoke up.

"I really came here Dad, Rev I mean; to tell you and the others that your friend Mac is dead. My contacts at Alpha Base said that the Colonel had left the base for a meeting with the General and his men gave Mac a cocktail of psychotropic drugs. They beat the living daylights out of him before they did this and then filled his system

with this stuff. All of it was per order directly from the Colonel!

They say he went through living hell, excuse my language; but that

is what it was. Some guards saw his body and said he was beaten to

a pulp and you could not recognize him. I am sorry for your loss Dad

and the loss to the others as well. But it is better that this crazy

Colonel Schmidt got Mac than you guys. "Tom stopped and saw

everyone looked devastated

"What do you mean Dead? He can't die!" Tiger fumed and Gin

sobbed at his side, the loss was too much. Then Tiger spoke as his

fury reach a pitch; "Uncle Mac dead, it couldn't be he survived other

stuff why not this?"

"I don't know Tiger, but Mac certainly saved our lives and for that

we are grateful" The Rev stopped, then suggested to them "let us

have a memorial for him tomorrow."

As the sun began its downward slide into the evening, sadness and

sorrow had more victims. By this time Cliff was nowhere to be

found and his dogs were with him. He was up high above the

overlook and in the woods where he and Mac spent time. He would

spend the night here with a fire and his dogs along with a bottle of scotch. He would remember Mac and think over all that he heard.

Anyhow it all seemed so strange that this Tom, the Rev's son knew

all this. If he wasn't the Rev's son, he would not trust him. But for

now, he would let it go. If Tom was responsible for Mac's death,

then Tom would die and Cliff would see to it. He would swear by

night's end that whoever did it to Mac; they would die a slow death

by the same method they used on Mac. Yes, they would die; or Cliff

would die trying to avenge Mac. Like the saying goes, when taking

revenge; dig two graves one for the person responsible and the other

one for you.

Cliff poured a scotch for Mac, in his absence; a drink was offered for

his friend. The drink would sit there until Cliff gave a toast to his

friend. Then Cliff would drink his and throw the other over his left

shoulder saying goodbye. The fire was hot and the night was cool.

Cliff was feeling the drink, and he was getting sadder as he drank. It

would be a long night, and with his dogs at his side; the glow of the

fire lit up the area. Pine trees around them stood as guards. A Night

owl hooted a lone call of urgency as the moon displayed itself on

this night. A night of remembrance and memorial to a friend, a close

friend! Cliff wished he had been there. How he wanted to be at

Mac's side at the moment of his passing. They were brothers, and brothers don't leave each other alone or to die. They help one another and in battle they watched each other's back. Cliff wondered how he could have done a better job to help Mac, but in the end, He had no answers, just memories of a good friend; one closer than a brother. He heart felt as if it had died as well, and he further drifted into a dark despair over the loss of his friend and brother in arms. Sometime in the early morning after much booze, Cliff wobbled on his feet as he lifted his glass up and said, "To my bro Mac, you will forever live on, brothers in life and comrades in death". Cliff saluted his glass to the empty place where the other drink for Mac was placed. Then Cliff went over to it, lifted it up and tossed the contents over his left shoulder and then threw the glass against the large pine standing off to one side of him.

Bravo Base two-one-niner was remarkably busy for so early in the morning. The word had been received from General Myers to move to the next level of Project Black Light. They now were working on Operation Viper and one of the targets was going to be Alpha base. The military was moving out people to other secret bases, which some believed were outside the USA. HAARP coordinates were set for the earthquake pinpointing Alpha base which would go through a deep tremor first, followed by severe shocks strong enough, as much as 8.5 on the Richter scale. That would do a lot of damage, but to make sure all areas, included reinforced bunkers were destroyed set explosive charges would coincide with the earthquake. All this would ensure that this base could never be used or entered again.

Bravo Base itself was being closed as well. Arrangements had been made for a military contractor to take over as soon as they had cleared out. As soon as this last series of HAARP incidents finished, they would dismantle the Bravo Base leaving only empty buildings for those coming in to utilize the facility. Many at Bravo base would transfer to the location in the rainforests of Brazil. Under a secret agreement that meant billions for Brazil, plus new jobs; the plan had been in place for many years. The State of the Art in Technology and Sciences are ready to be utilized. Only now was the project revealed and plans have been already going on to move all personal there quickly but covertly. The public would never be aware of this.

"Yes General Myers we are ready and have the coordinates. I will be ready to leave Bravo Base tonight and will fly with my staff to the new location. Our people will have the system totally dismantled within a month and in six months the new HAARP with the new beast mega-system computer will be ready. We have already been working on the new faster light computer, we call the beast. Sir it is generations ahead of anything that is out there now", The C.O. finished and listened

"Good Brad, I want to be notified the minute you start the process for Alpha base. Keep in touch" The General stopped and welcomed Brad Peterson into the fold of this new world system. Brad whole heartedly saw the light so to speak some time ago and since then he had been on a trial basis. He had passed with flying colors.

The Colonel hung up the phone and looked out the window. It was lush, green, and the best weather there is. But the new assignment is to the next level. Never has such a HAARP system been combined with a light pulse computer, this is unlike anything out there. The capabilities, speed, and ability of this system would be unlimited and he, Lieutenant Colonel Peterson would also get promoted and a new job. Much more pay, more rank, and many more kudos. His family would be safely ushered out of America waiting for the next phase of Black Light to happen and then finish.

He smiled and listened to the birds singing their songs. He was happy today, although he was one of those working on the downfall of an America that he had not liked for some time. Now he was with people that would bring in the nation that this land deserved. He had a front row seat and stood to gain when it was all finished.

The room was dark and strange noises seemed to be all around him. Mac had his eyes closed and listened for a very long time to try to get an idea of what was going on and where he was at. He remembered his dreams, nightmares, and all the stuff. He knew right away what it was, drugs! They had given him psychotropic drugs and probably meant to drive him mad or kill him. But he was alive, or was he. Mac gingerly opened one eye and immediately a face was close to his own and the smell was horrid. But Mac grinned; he would know that smell and face anywhere.

"Noah, what are you doing?" Mac weakly exclaimed

"Me taking care of my buddy Mac that is you" Noah was huge, and in the right place he was a killer, an assassin, but he was also loyal. All the hybrid Nephilim were, Mac forgot the new name the scientists had laid on them. These were humanlike, but big.

"Noah, thanks for the help, is there a bathroom around here, I got to get up and go?" Mac moved and noticed his shoulder felt better; in fact, his whole body was better. He looked at Noah and asked, "How long have I been here?" Not waiting, Mac went to the restroom and then came out after a few minutes looking at Noah for the answer.

"Noah not know, but long-time boss!" Noah finished and looked outside the room as Dorothy came in, she smiled and said "You are finally awake, we almost lost you. Several times you were at the edge. Someone must have been praying, not that I am a believer; but really Mac, it is a miracle you survived that gob of drugs they gave you. If we had not of shown up to give you something to stop them, we would be planting you. Colonel Schmidt was told you died, there is a grave with a body in it, but it isn't you. It is so disfigured that they would not be able to tell the difference. The word has gone out that you died Mac.

Mac looked at Dorothy and was glad to see her. "Dorothy thanks for getting me out!"

"Well I wanted to get you out the minute I saw you come in, but there was no way. But the brass in the Pentagon heard what Schmidt was doing and they stopped it. This base is targeted for destruction"

Dorothy stopped as Mac spoke up "and the Colonel, Schmidt I mean; what of him?"

"I have not heard but those in the know have secretly let out he is on the short list. They will retire him and make sure he is not heard from again, if you catch my drift", Dorothy smiled and looked at Mac who was frowning, and then she asked him "What is the Matter Mac? I thought you would be glad he was given up?"

"I am it is just that I want to finish him, I owe him Dorothy!" Mac gritted his teeth and clinched his fist at the thought of not being able to kill the Colonel

"Right now, you can't fight your way out of a paper bag and you want to take care of Schmidt. Oh, that's a great idea, are you crazy or is it you just have a death wish Mac" Dorothy stopped and then jokingly laughed at the thought of Mac actually doing it

"I know, I know, but it is still bothersome" Mac stopped, and then yawned.

"Right now, you need some sleep; I will have Noah close all the curtains and the door, so you can get rest. You will need it when we move out." Dorothy stopped and touched Mac lightly, "You know Mac I love you, don't you?" She bent over and kissed him on the cheek, then moved her mouth gently over his lips, and they kissed a long deep kiss.

The perfume Dorothy had on wafted around Macs head and into his nostrils. The scent was driving him crazy, if only he could just grab her now, but as he began to get into the long kiss; she withdrew with a laugh and said "Not now big boy that is just an appetizer. You get well Mac and hurry up. I won't wait forever; I have waited for you long enough." And with that Dorothy took Noah outside the room after closing the curtains. Noah stood his guard and no one came within twenty feet of him or he would scowl and grit his teeth. No one, not even others of his kind would mess with Noah on his mission. Right now, Noah was busy and his mission was keeping his friend Mac safe, he would do that and anyone who came close would die. You could bet on that and everyone knew Noah and feared him.

Mac had been sleep for a long time, but suddenly he awoke with a start. Mac sat up some and looked around. The room was dark and silent. He was alone, and then out of the corner came a bearded man, with a hat, and coat on. He smiled at Mac and said, "Hi Mac"

"Who are you?" Mac looked at him but did not recognize him

"I am called the Prophet, but in some parts I am nicknamed the sagebrush prophet." The Prophet smiled as he looked at Mac and said, "the Lord sent me."

"You mean like the Old Testament Prophets we all heard about in Sunday school?" Mac exclaimed

"Yes Mac, I am just as the Prophets of old, and I believe in Jesus, Yeshua HaMassiach. The Lord appeared to you as a bright shining light and broke up the visions you were having from the drugs. It was him who stopped the poison from killing you. I am here to tell you that the vision is real; the Lord Jesus Christ is alive and well. He has called you. You also called out for the Lord to save you. Mac, he has heard you. All you need to do is receive him, John chapter one says that "as many as received him, to them gave he power to become the sons of God. John chapter three says "ye must be born again of the spirit. Just believe on him Mac and you will be saved." The Prophet stopped and looked at Mac who seemed as if he couldn't believe what was happening

"How did you get in here Prophet", Mac asked, then added "Noah would have killed you if he saw you"

"I come and go as the wind, the Lord places me where he wants me Mac, besides Noah would not touch me Mac, I am the Prophet and I have angels standing guard around me as I speak." The Prophet finished

Noah heard talking in the room and opened the door. He saw Mac talking to someone and Noah was mad. He did not know who it was, but Noah was going to kill them. As he moved into the room, his fury was evident.

Mac saw Noah and knew he was mad and Mac shouted, "Watch out Prophet, Noah will kill you"

The Prophet turned around and saw Noah, held up his hand and immediately Noah stopped.

"Noah not hurt Prophet, not hurt Prophet, sorry" Noah turned his head and walked out calmly

"You see Mac, I am a Prophet and anointed of the Lord to do his will." The Prophet stopped and saw Mac looking at him

"Amazing prophet I have known Noah longer than anyone and never have I seen him go from fury to kill to calm and saying he is sorry, never Prophet, never have I seen this before" Mac stopped

The Prophet expounded scriptures of the Messiah from Moses, the Prophets, to the New Testament. He summed it up by saying, "Mac you must firmly believe that Jesus Christ came into this world born of a virgin, that he gave testimony of the Father and presented the gospel. He declared he was the Way, the Truth, and the Life. He was crucified on the cross for our sins, and was resurrected from the dead. He was seen alive of many infallible proofs and witnesses even as many as five hundred at once. He Left instructions for the church, ascended into heaven, is at the right hand of the Father, and is coming again."

"That was in my vision, the bright white light blocked out all other visions and lights, and the voice said I am the Way, the Truth, and the Life Prophet, that is what he said of himself." Mac stopped

"Well Mac, you must believe in your heart that Jesus Christ is Lord, the Only Son of God, that he died for your sins, and was raised from the dead the third day. Then confess your sins and repent by following him." The Prophet stopped and saw Mac with a tear

"Prophet in the hell I went through and in the hatred, I had to avenge; I came to know one thing. It is no good. In all of that I only wanted peace. In that vision and hearing that voice I felt peace and love as I have never felt it Prophet. I mean never! I want that peace"

Mac stopped, his heart was pounding and he felt like it would burst.

With that the Prophet led Mac in prayer and soon the two hugged

and the prophet blessed him. Then the Prophet said "Mac let me pray

for you, you must be healed and ready to walk out of here. When

you leave here go to Cliffs Ranch, everyone you know is there. Let

the Rev tell you what you need to do in learning more about your

new faith."

The Prophet prayed and moved his hands, without touching Mac

over all his body. Mac felt a strange sensation, and heat began in his

head and moved throughout his body. It then came to rest in his heart

area. But then electricity seemed to move throughout his body as he

felt hot surges flowing into his body. He began moving the parts of

his body that hurt.

"There Mac, believe, and stand in the Promise, scripture gives us

concerning our Lord; as Peter says "by his stripes we were healed.

Arise Mac, stand up and claim your healing"

Mac moved to the side of the bed and gingerly stood up, he felt

unsteady at first. Then like adrenalin, a surge of strength shot

through his body. He was hot in all his body, and a power, a force moved over him like a wind. He felt no pain in his shoulders or feet, matter of fact; there was no pain at all!

"I feel great Prophet, I believe Prophet, today I believe" Mac stopped, and then frowned

The Prophet saw him frown and said, "you will have to forgive him Mac, if you do not forgive him, the Lord cannot forgive you!"

"The Colonel, you want me to forgive that idiotic murdering fool? I cannot forgive him Prophet, can I? How can I forgive such a bloody man?" Mac stopped and paused.

"Mac the Lord forgave you and you had much blood on your hands, were you not called Murder incorporated? Were you not proud of that? No, Mac you must forgive and the Lord will give you his grace Mac, his favor to do this!" the Prophet stopped

"Okay Prophet, I will try, but it is hard" Mac stopped and prayed

"Oh Lord help me to forgive the Colonel"

"There Mac, you will make it, I must be going" The Prophet stopped and went to the door, taking one last look, he went out. The curtain had blocked Mac's view so he rushed out of the room.

"Where is he Noah, where did he go?" Mac excitedly shouted

"Gone Mac, Prophet is with God, he goes?" Noah stopped and was silent

"What door Noah, where did he go" Mac persisted

"He no go through door Mac, he disappear, poof, he gone; Noah see and then Noah not see Prophet; he gone Mac, to God Mac; he is Prophet, mighty Prophet, this Noah can tell you Mac, he mighty man; no mess with Prophet!"

Mac went back into his room and was overjoyed and as he went to his bed, there was a book. It was signed, "Welcome Mac, my brother into Gods Kingdom, read the book of John first and have faith, pray to the Lord Jesus, and believe Mac." It was signed "The Sagebrush Prophet."

Chapter Ten: Downfall

How art thou fallen from heaven, O Lucifer, son of the morning!

how art thou cut down to the ground, which didst weaken the nations

Isaiah 14:12

Colonel Schmidt was back on the bullet train and heading back to

his office at Alpha base. His meeting with the General was strange.

The General called him back to the base to cover basic operations of

the base and nothing else. All of it could have been handled on the

phone. To make matters worse, in his absence; Mac had died. He

wanted to see the body, but he had been told that his face was

unrecognizable and the body already buried. He was mad; he had

wanted Mac to suffer more. He wanted to stretch it out. But the

cocktail of drugs he had told the guards to give him was his own

recipe. The Colonel prided himself in this. However, he had wanted

to personally see how Mac reacted to it. But when the General calls, you must answer. No matter what goes on, being loyal to the rank is paramount in this business. There is no doubt, he thought; the guards got carried away with Mac. He would properly discipline them himself when he got back, but that would wait for other items on his agenda. Mac was now dead; he was happy and now was moving to eradicate the others in this nest of trouble makers. Still despite it all, the Colonel was bothered, no he was troubled over the meeting with the General and about Macs death; yet he couldn't pinpoint it exactly. Something strange was going on and it surrounded him. He did not like it. Was it an ambush? It surely felt like he was being set up, but in this business, you had to take risks. He had done that all his life and always won. Nothing made him think that this time, maybe he would lose out!

He had for some time been monitoring various groups. He had men wiretap various phone companies. They were experts in hacking into the company's mainframe and setting up a 'soft-wire' tap. This would provide remote observation where his men could then allow the infected software to run a program that would give them all the metadata they needed. By running the system through their own computers, they could narrow down the information and find people that fit their keyword description. In this case, Remnant, Patriots, Christian, and have special names like Mac in the keywords to identify anyone mentioned in such a conversation. They had picked up communication about Mac's death going over the wires. They recorded the location, conversation, and other relevant data. One of these locations was in Wyoming. It was connected to another name he knew, which was Cliff. They had the location and now he would personally oversee hitting Cliff's location.

As the bullet train pulled into Alpha base, he looked around. His men stood at attention as he walked off the ramp and took the elevator going up to his office. He stepped out and walked into the hall to his office, then opened the door and saw the stack of papers and mail waiting for him. But as he sat down, he quickly turned around to look out the window. He saw the vast desert stretch out before him and the blue sky above. The hills were in the distance and the whole area looked quiet. Just as he liked, this was the quiet solitude of the desert. But he thought of George Washington, no doubt he would not be a friend but an enemy! Good old George, he did say things that made sense. He then remembered the warning Washington had given, of the danger of governmental power. It was

George Washington the Father of this nation, the Colonel smiled and seemed amused. It was him who said "Government is not reason, it is not eloquence; it is force! Like fire, it is a dangerous servant and a fearful master". Yes, by George; you are right and I am now that force! No one has ever accused the Colonel of being eloquent, but dangerous, yes. Like fire, I Colonel Schmidt and those with me make a fearful master; we have force and will use it.

No one was sure if the Colonel knew that the C.A.C.F. had been given orders. But at night the crafts had been moving everything. The UFO buffs had been located some miles away watching the night sky. They were excited at all the recent activity and had no idea what was really happening. Moving for the C.A.C.F. was simple, really. For these Aliens in this section of Alpha base their ships, or UFO's as the humans called them, carried all they had. Plus here was where the undefined species as human scientists called them, made their home. They came and went as they pleased without human interference. Now they would have a new home. But this was not the only base, this was the Central Command. Other such bases were around the world. Main bases were in Germany, Russia, China, Indonesia, America, Antarctica, and now in Brazil. The last species was located in the off-limit's section. They were reptilians and lived underground. The labs there would be destroyed and the reptilians would move themselves underground. This was their home and rarely did they go to the surface. The explosion would not harm them, they simply would move further underground and away from the location where they were now at. The Pleiadean's lived for the most part among humans and in the other area of level 13. The Scientists had targeted three kinds of Alien species that were humanoid. The Pleiadean's, the Nephilim, and the Ascended Masters all of whom are extraterrestrial but all look like or close to humanoid. But the Pleiadean's and Nephilim were the only ones who worked closely with the project and could walk among the public. The Ascended Masters were enlightened ones who came and went as they chose. No one really knew where they came from, but they had a mission like the Pleiadean's, that is to bring mankind to a higher consciousness of their own Godhood.

Dorothy, Noah, Mac, and some other soldiers of Pickett's headed out the dock from which the Aliens had been leaving. It was about Eleven pm and the evening dusk had settled bringing with it night. There were four Humvee's waiting in the darkness for the group.

They moved up the steel walkway to the surface. The night sky came into view as they stepped on the top cover of the transport area which had moved, uncovering the space beneath it. The cover literally hid a huge Alien city, space craft, and government labs. But soon all this would-be history. Well placed charges would go off, then huge dirt movers and machines would cover this place up and replant it with native plants. Soon, no one could ever tell what was under it. The cover itself was a huge steel structure with sturdy grids underneath and a top of desert floor, complete with dirt, fauna, cacti, and other items that made it blend in with the desert itself. All of it was surrounded by miles and miles of off limit area. No one could get close and snipers were set at intervals along with security to keep everyone out. The only way in was the highway which came right up to the gate and the guardhouse. When the base was finally closed the area would be under watch. However, they also would salt some of the outlying area with uranium and then put up signs about dangerous radiation. This would keep trespassers out. Although everything would be destroyed and covered, they still did not want strangers lurking about.

Mac was feeling good as they now walked on pure desert floor. He looked up and saw the massive expanse of the desert sky. It was not too long ago that seeing such a sight and being free seemed impossible. Ahead of him were Noah and another Nephilim who took the lead. Their senses were very acute and it was impossible, practically for anything to sneak up on them. Their eyesight was also very keen as was their hearing. But it was possible to kill Nephilim, even with all their sensory abilities and physical skills. Soldiers took up both sides, the rear, and just behind Noah. Dorothy walked beside Mac.

"Mac, I am amazed at how fast you healed! It was just a miracle, although I don't understand how you got well so fast, I am glad you did. You really look 100% my man, yes you look like you are your old self" Dorothy stopped speaking and then listened as a Coyote howled in the desert night. She tilted her head and looked around saying to Mac "Hear that, I love the cry of the Coyote, so free, so distant, and crying out for you to listen to them."

"Well, it is great tonight; I also like the sounds of the desert at night. Believe me, I am glad I feel better as well, and again, thanks for getting me out. As for me feeling good and being 100%, I tell you that the Lord sent his Prophet and healed me." Mac stopped and looked at Dorothy, who was shaking her head. He knew this was too much for her.

"Mac, I do not believe in all that stuff. I mean I want too, but listen. I was raised in a Congregational church. I was raised with Jesus and his father; you know the Easter and Christmas stories. Well I knew them all. But when my mother got sick, I prayed, I mean I prayed a lot. She died of breast cancer and along with that also died my faith Mac" Dorothy stopped and a tear came to her eye remembering her mom, then she said "Besides if Jesus really exists, and God is a god of love, why did my mom die? She was a good woman, hardworking, and loved her family. Why Mac? Dorothy pulled up and grabbed his arm, she saw him looking at her.

"Dorothy, I do not know. All I can tell you is what happened to me! I do know that there is an answer and one day we all will know, especially you as to why these things happen to people we love." Mac stopped and grabbed her as she melted in his arms. Dorothy, don't worry; everything will be alright.

Mac let Dorothy go and they saw the vehicles ahead and around them several people. One of whom he knew right away. He ran up and looked closer.

"Ace how are you? It has been a very long time you old reprobate! Mac stopped as he saw Ace smile. "You are still a pain in the butt Mac; I am always getting you out of trouble! Can't you just stay out of this and take it easy?" Ace laughed and grabbed Mac, and then said, "How are you brother, long time no see!"

"Ace, my brother, I have truly missed you since those days we were growing up together. The two twin brothers hugged one another and in those moments of silence, the bond was evident.

 It has been many miles, how are the family?" Mac stopped

"Well, they are the reason I came, but first; we arrived in time to save the Rev and his people, although they had lost some men by the time we made it. They are now at another location." Ace stopped and looked serious at Mac, then said "Mac they want you home, Dad is dead; mom is sick. But I reminded them of the "Circle and our responsibilities".

"I would love to see them, but right now I must get back with Cliff and the others", Mac stopped as Ace shouted in, saying "That's it, they went to Cliffs; that is the name"

"Mac, it was General Myers who made sure there was a rescue plan for you" Dorothy looked at both Ace and Mac, then said "you guys are identical, how did they ever tell you apart!" Both Ace and Mac looked at her and smiled; then Mac answered saying "only I have the birth mark over my right nipple. Mac continued as he looked at Ace once again "Good General Myers, yes Myers and I got along very well. It is good to have people on your side, people in high places, but also the power of my "family."

"You are right on that count as well, Myers also said that it was that reason, the power of your "Guardians" that made those in the project think twice before doing anything to you, they did not want to mess with them. When we get to the main road the soldiers will head to Colonel Pickett's and get ready for the phase of Viper." Ace finished as everyone began getting in.

Noah, Mac, Dorothy, Ace, and one of his men got in one Humvee. They drove the long drive out of the area. As the desert passed by, the night made its way toward early morning. There was much to talk about and Ace and Mac had not seen each other in many, many years. Now it was time to enjoy each other while they could. They remembered their boyhood and the passing of the torch to them as leaders in the "Guardians" and the fight they were to take on.

The ceremony was over and there was not a dry eye left, it seemed. The Rev had finished the benediction, and now led the group away from a grave. The headstone was marked, Mac "a friend in life and a brother in death." There was no body, so the grave was empty. This made them even angrier. They wanted a body at least, to bring closure; you needed a body. But, no body was to come, that is; as they expected. Cynthia and the women made a potluck and set up the tables in one of the outbuildings. The line formed and in it were friends of Mac and Cliff. Cliff had called them in for the ceremony. Most had heard through the grapevine that Mac died. In all there were about eighty people in that outbuilding with many of them former black ops, soldiers, and friends that knew Mac and operated in the same arena he did. Every one of them had told Cliff, they were ready to go to the hilt, to plunge the knife of vengeance deep into the Colonel and his men for doing this. Little did they know that before the day was over, it would come to pass? They would have this chance, but for many of them; death would come quick.

As the guards looked out over Cliff's ranch, the scene was quiet. The day was not too hot, and the pines provided good shade for them. As they looked out, two shots rang out from sniper's rifle's in the distance. Shots that were on target and muzzled, no sound; death was silent and quick. The forest around Cliffs Ranch was thick and the shade provided cover for men who now kneeled beside the Colonel, as he signaled with his fist. Silently the men spread out; they were heavily armed and ready for anything. The road was blocked by a very official government agency van with the words FBI on the side. Two other cars with similar insignia's sit at the side of the road with men alongside them. They look like typical government FBI types and they were making sure no one can get near the area. All traffic was being re-routed away from Cliff's ranch.

In the outbuilding the meal was not yet over, everyone had gone through the line for food. But most of them sat chatting with each other. A man comes in from outside and goes to Cliff, he is moving quickly. He whispers something and Cliff gets up. Soon the place is filled with soft whispers as Cliff rolls out a large container on wheels. He opens the top and starts handing out ammo and rifles. Another case is brought out and twenty clip autos are given out with holsters to men and women. Sniper rifles are then seen and a few of the men take them and load them up. They handle them like they knew what they were doing. Pretty soon the men head out trying to hide from view the arms and make their way to other buildings. The Snipers climb high up in the crow's nest of the barn and out of sight, begin scoping out the area. They get on the radios Cliff gave them and report; "Enemy sighted, about 1000 yards and closing. They are all around, professionals it looks like. Well let's give them a reception they will not forget." As the place quiets down, women with pistols take the children with them below the outbuilding where they had been eating. It had a basement of sorts, with a door that is hard to find. It lifts up from the floor and closes again. Men scatter straw around to hide the door and with a few of the women who chose to fight, including Cynthia. They all take up secure positions. Cliff stands in the outbuilding and Cynthia is at his side. He takes his sniper rifle and scopes the area. He hears a silent thud as a bullet hits the door panel beside him. He stands aside and looks at the Rev across the opening from him. He motions to the Rev to get down.

The Rev takes his rifle and aims carefully and lets loose.

"Got him" The Rev said, "Over there in the shade of the woods, to

the south a bit, a sniper"

"Yes I see another one" Cliff aims and pulls the trigger, with a jolt

the rifle sends it message, a hard jacket steel armor piercing shell

hits someone in the distance and they go down.

The firing begins in earnest as the Colonels men closes in. They are

firing autos and some have AK's, they move swiftly firing. They

have the Ranch surrounded and now are making sure no one can

escape through any holes in their positions.

The Rev continues to fire and see's several of the men lying around

dead. Already they have taken many casualties. He picks another

target and shoots, it goes down. He does this again and again as the

battle heats up.

Cynthia was taught to shoot by her dad and now is using a standard

30-06. It has open sights and has a five-cartridge holding capacity in

it. She fires at various targets, wounding one in the leg and sending

another one down screaming.

But as the bullets fly, more of those defending Cliffs Ranch go down. The Colonel is in the field crouching and watches it as he grabs his rifle and squeezes the trigger.

Tom the Rev's son goes down in a heap and rolls on the ground. He is seriously wounded and now Cynthia sees him as he lay in an open doorway. She grabs another person and they run and grab Tom by the arms pulling him out of sight. In the corner Cynthia opens his shirt, he is bleeding badly, soon one of the men rush to her side. He looks at her and says "I am a medic, or was, I will take over; get me some alcohol, bandages, and towels. If you do have a medic kit, get that and bring it fast."

"We have medic kits; there are several in the ammo box over there." Cynthia stops speaking and runs to get the kit, she gives it to the Medic and then says, "you have it under control, will he live?"

He looks up and nods an affirmative, then says "Yes, but it is bad. I must stop the bleeding. I can also take out the bullet; have some people get a table, hot water, etc. I will take good care of him", The Medic stopped talking and began to stop the bleeding as he prepared to take out the bullet, just like the firefights he had known so many years ago.

Cynthia ran to the Rev's side and looked at Cliff who by now had stopped firing to reload a clip. But soon he was again picking targets. They had gotten quite a few of them, but they kept coming. Cliff was not sure how long they could hold out.

As Cliff looked out he saw men going down in the field. At first he thought his group were killing them, but soon he realized that Gunfire was coming from somewhere other than the main Ranch house and outbuilding area. The Fire was from the trees.

The Colonel also saw the men going down and turned around. As he did, horror struck him. He was now being surrounded by soldiers, who they are he did not know but they were shooting and killing his men. He turned around and gave orders to some of the men to pick targets behind them. But they fell as they did. The Colonel picked his targets and shot, the men went down. He was deadly in a firefight and now he fought like all the demons in hell were summoned.

He hit the ground as more fire came his way and he crawled to the edge of the tree line. He stood up quickly behind a large pine and scoped the area. He was outnumbered. His men was making headway against those at the Ranch, but now; they were losing and badly. As he put down his glasses he saw his men in hand to hand combat and fighting valiantly.

"Well, well Colonel; good day for a stroll" The voice was familiar and the Colonel growled, "Mac, you Son of a Bitch"

"Well good to see you as well, you foul mouthed piece of trash", Mac stopped himself "You don't know how long I waited to get your lousy carcass alone so I could kill you"

The Colonel knew trouble and this was trouble. He never would want to meet Mac alone, but now after he had tortured him, here he was. "How did you get well so fast?"

"The Lord Colonel, the Lord sent his Prophet; you know the Lord, Jesus Christ" I am his servant now, Mac stopped and saw the Colonel turn red

"Jesus, Jesus, you accepted that no good false god, Mac the true god is Lucifer, I serve him and he owns this world" The Colonel stopped, having been interrupted.

"Colonel despite what you did to me, I forgive you, but I will kill you; it is only justice" Mac stopped

"You will never kill me Mac, the Lord Lucifer reigns and I am his right-hand man here. I run this show to bring in his kingdom!"

"You are finished Colonel and so are your ways, I am the one who will kill you dead as a rock and the devil is your undertaker" Mac now snarled and raised his rifle and pulled the trigger; it jammed, The Colonel laughed, and saw his chance as he raised his auto and pointed it directly at Mac, and then he laughed loud, so loud it drowned out the gunfire in the distance just for a moment. This was a shrill which went through the forest around them. "Mac, you are done, I wanted to be there to watch you die; now I will finish what I started. I wanted you on my team, but no; you wouldn't come. It is your fault you will be dead Mac. You could have seen the glorious kingdom Lucifer is bringing in, but not now. I will on the other hand see it and reign with him."

As the Colonel pointed the weapon his finger slowly was pulling the trigger, then a noise startled both him and Mac.

Mac looked over and saw the Prophet standing there, the Colonel saw him and growled, "You"

"Yes Colonel, me; or should I say I have come in the name of the Real Lord, the name of Yeshua; Jesus Christ", the Prophet looked at Mac and said, "behold the glory and power of the Lord"! The prophet waved his hand and the earth began moving and the Colonel fell as Mac steadied himself on the Pine tree close by. Then with a finger the Prophet pointed at the Colonel and said, "In the Name of the Yeshua; Jesus Christ, be it done unto thee as you purposed to do to others!"

With that the Colonel grabbed his heart, his eyes sunk in his head and he dropped like a rock. Then the earth opened and a foul odor of sulfur came out of the ground and the Colonel fell in and immediately the earth closed again.

"Mac how are you doing, I am glad to see you out of the Alpha base", The Prophet smiled and came close to Mac, they shook hands and Mac said "Thanks" and looked at the Prophet.

"I could not let you kill him; he was to meet his justice according to his fruits. It is enough that you forgave him, but you could not kill him. I meted out justice in the Name of the Lord." The Prophet looked at him and turned to go, "I must leave now, tell the others how the Colonel died"

Mac looked down at where the Colonel was standing and then back to the Prophet to say goodbye, but he was gone. "How does he do that?" Mac was left wondering, but left it to the Lords doing.

The battle was over. Everyone was now grouped together with Tiger, Gin, the Rev, and Cynthia standing out in front of the barn. Cliff came up alongside them and they all looked in the distance. The group could not believe their eyes. By now Ace had joined Mac and the two brothers, unbeknown to them being twins, saw two Mac's. As the two identical figures came close the only thing that separated the two was the military black garb of one of them. It was then, as shock wore off that they all exclaimed "Two of you, how could that be?"

The two looked at each other and grinned as they turned to those looking at them, then they said together "twins!" Mac saw Cliff and raised his hand saying, "Cliff my friend, it is Mac."

"Mac, you are alive", with that Cliff ran to him and grabbed his friend, "Man am I glad to see you again, you know I even toasted your death with a fifth of Scotch! You both are identical, but how?" Cliff stopped short and Mac interrupted him and grabbed Ace; "Cliff and everyone meet my brother Ace and as we said earlier; we are identical Twins."

Everyone was still a bit stunned. They now stood looking at two people who were identical except for their voices and a slight difference in eye color, but for all intents and purposes; you would never know these are two different people. After a lull of a couple of minutes, everyone started to speak again and headed across the yard to the house chatting as they went.

As the group gathered around to hear from Mac and his escape a huge wave of horror came over some of them. "What is that?"

"Those look like the ones who hit us at the Ranch, quick get the guns" the Rev shouted

"Wait Rev, these are friendlies here; they are on your side!" Mac smiled as the Rev and a few others put down the guns.

"Mac, me kill Colonels men. Noah no like Colonel. Noah see what bad Colonel did to good friend Mac" Noah came up with his compatriot Nephilim.

"They look just like humans, except they are big; real big. They look mean Mac" said Gin in Amazement

"Well, they are part human, and today genetics has helped them even more" Mac stopped

"They can be formidable enemies, but Noah and I have been friends since he came to Alpha Base. Matter of fact, I got along with all of them. But they are also formidable friends. They will not let you down if you treat them right and are honest." Mac stopped and slapped Noah on the back, "thanks Noah for your help, Mac likes friend Noah and Nephilim."

"Noah and other Nephilim like Mac and his friends, we go now, will join later" Noah and the other Nephilim walked away slowly and were soon out of sight in the woods.

The evening came as Ace's men took the bodies and the vehicles away. The cleanup was done and everyone sat around glad that Mac was alive.

"I can't believe I have two uncles" Tiger exclaimed, "You guys look identical, I bet no one can tell you two apart" with that Tiger stopped as he heard, "Yes there is a difference, I'm smarter" coming from both Mac and Ace; who then looked at each other and laughed. "But there is a difference and when you grow up I will let you in on the secret," with that Mac looked at his nephew and knew he would not stop asking until he made Mac tell him. But for now the secret would be safe.

"I have one other thing Mac", the Rev asked; "How did they find us all this time!"

"I can help Dad, I tried to intervene on your behalf when I overheard the Colonel issuing hit orders on the Ranch!" the Rev turned around and saw Tom

"What did you do exactly?" The Rev asked

"Well, I asked the Colonel to spare you and your group" Tom stopped and saw everyone looking at him. "I told him that it was too dangerous to keep on making raids and killing people. I told him of the word from higher command was that there was too much chaos going on, they wanted it peaceful. Well the Colonel knew that higher-ups did not like his methods but he could not be persuaded to stop his aggressive tactics. He was doing this on his own, the way he always had done, this he told me with a smile. The guy loves blood and murder; I am glad to be rid of him. But I never told him a thing about the Ranch, its location, or the people; he already knew it all and I have no clue as to how!" I can only surmise that the Colonel must have followed me, but I was very careful; besides how had known I was a double agent?"

The Rev Smiled and looked relieved and said "Tom I had thought of you and was worried that somehow you were the mole in the group the Prophet talked about! But as I think about the Prophet's own words, he did not refer to a mole or to a person; he said, 'betrayal had found its way' into the group and that someone I knew was involved. I assumed the betrayer was a person I knew, but it was a bug that the Colonel used to gather the information. He used it on someone I knew and loved and that someone had no clue.""!

Upon hearing the discussion, Mac moved forward as he looked at Tom; "You did not give the group up nor did he follow you; he did not have too! Bring me your cell phone" Mac looked at him and reached out for the phone, Mac opened up the back, pulled out some wires and took his pocket knife and within a few moments held up a small black object.

"This friend is what many in my profession call a 'remob' or remote observation piece. It is easy for our people to hack into mainframes of phone companies to set up a wiretap. They install software on the mainframe which utilizes the ability to hack the system, record information and metadata. They can track the location of anyone." Mac looked at everyone and then proceeded; this bug here is another device that is used, especially by the Colonel. He will at a whim automatically bug those under him. It will record everything and send it to another receiver. However, there are limitations with this bug, they must be close enough to receive it. They must have bugged your phone as an extra precaution. But they can also install what is called a 'black virus' on your cell phone. This is the most likely way your information got into the Colonel's hands. They simply hack your phone the way you hack a computer. Although, it is easier because most cell phones do not have firewalls or even the simplest security features. They put the virus in the phone and call the infected phone by putting in a security code to trigger the virus. When they call your phone, it doesn't ring, the call doesn't show up on your phone, and the phones microphone is turned on. Then they can eavesdrop on your conversation and then follow-up with the wiretap. What makes this so user friendly is the person being recorded has no clue. Even if you do find out your being recorded, it is very hard, next to impossible to trace who did it!"

Mac Continued "Tiger have you been listening"

"Yes, Mac I have", Tiger responded

"Then you are appointed our chief of security over these types of things. Do you think you can prevent such things from happening again?" Mac asked

"Yes, Mac I sure can and I can find resources to make sure our communications are safe, but I will need help" Tiger stopped

"I will help; I need to learn the stuff; after all they tapped my phone!" Tom stopped and looked at Mac

"I want to help as well" Gin responded

"You both will do just fine and Tom, this stuff happens to best of us, even Ace and I have had such simple taps on our phone." Mac Laughed, then added "the Lord was watching over us all"

Everyone smiled and knew that they indeed had heaven watching over them and they were thankful for that.

"Listen everyone", Ace held up his secure sat phone and said "repeat"

"Sir Alpha base is destroyed. An earthquake went off some time ago and at the same moment the charges went off. The Base is down, I repeat it is down. The movers are covering the last remaining vestiges. All buildings are being removed, dirt is being hauled in and the place reseeded."

With that everyone cheered! "We did it, with a little help from our friends!"

The group sat around, this time with a large roaring fire and steaks were brought out along with drinks.

Cliff and Mac sat around the fire and looked as Ace was busy talking to Tiger. "He has had a lot of me Cliff, but Tiger has not had much of Ace. Tiger will keep pumping him for information until Ace leaves"

They both smiled as the evening was greeted by the roaring fire and the pines settled into the night. The fields around Cliffs place were also getting back to normal after all the racket that went on. The critters of the night stood around watching the party of humans and the fire which danced in the night.

Mac patted Cliff on the shoulder and then moved to Dorothy's side, "let's go for a walk, shall we?"

Dorothy looked at Mac nodding. They walked to the edge of the forest and then up the hill, holding hands and enjoying each other. Mac took her to the top of the ridge, a short walk. They both stood there and looked out over the area.

As they left, they saw Tiger and Gin cuddling each other by the large roaring fire. Mac said "look at those two" Dorothy saw them both and smiled "yes love is in the air Mac" with that Dorothy squeezed Mac tighter to her.

"It is beautiful Mac, the stars are bright, the milky way is spreading across the sky, and look there goes a streak of light, Mac; there goes one of our friends"

"Mac laughed and said, UFO; yes, on their way to a rainforest in Brazil. It is an amazing night and a wonderful life. And Dorothy I must also tell you more about Jesus."

"You know Mac, I like the new you! Yes, I want to hear about this Jesus that you serve!" Dorothy looked up at the sky and held onto Mac, who by now was cuddling her close "I like this Mac, surely I do; you know I love you, did I ever tell you I love you?"

"Yes, you have, and while we are at it. Have I told you before that I love you?" Mac answered with a lump in this throat

"Not ever Mac, Not once" Dorothy quipped smiling

"Well, my dear Dorothy, I love you, yes indeed" with that he pulled her close as his nostrils welcomed the perfume on her neck. He drew close and as he did, his heart pounded and an excitement welled up inside. Dorothy began to shiver slightly and moved closer anticipating his embrace. They touched lips gingerly, and then they embraced a deep embrace as the two lovers kissed. The stars danced and the campfire played out its role, as Dorothy and Mac were kissing deeply.

Then, they separated and Dorothy looked at him, "Mac is this over yet?"

"No, my dear, it is not!" Mac stopped and then said, "But tonight, for you and me, it is over; let us talk of other things and a future."

"Yes Mac, I like this other you, No I love this other you even more than the other Mac." Dorothy stopped and silently watched the night with Mac. Two lone sentries' in the night, two star crossed lovers meeting by chance, but people who had gone through much together. Two people whose destinies' entwined during a fight with people who sought to Steel the Darkness. Two people whose lives crossed paths into the faith and testimony of Jesus Christ.

Epilogue:

Ace had returned to his duties working with the Guardians and was glad he saw his twin Mac. The two had been separated by destiny and a plan. This plan was to have Guardians of America in place from the time of George Washington, which were the roots. But it was fully tested during Lincoln's assassination and during the

successive war. A plan which followed an open vision that George

Washington had and one that Washington shared with the First head

of the Guardians.

But into the historical fight comes both heaven and hell raging on the

shores and in the plains of America. A destiny at stake and a people

that are blinded, two sides wage war for the purpose to which they

are dedicated.

It is here that the battle rages, in the hearts of men and women in the

many states which are united under one flag in a place called

America. Over the years many have shed blood on distant shores for

the cause of the flag and the constitution which many hold dear. But

there is a new breed now, one with powers from the oval office, to

the Pentagon, and into the principalities of darkness. It stretches out

from there into every corner of America. However, there stands

staunch opposition between darkness and their purpose. This

opposition is the Guardians, a group from the dawn of this nation

and carried through to this day. With them also stands a Remnant of

Americans who will fight and die for the cause of which the nation

stands for.

The Prophet stood to the side of the car, the red desert stretched out before him. Benjamin was alongside and watching a car drive up. The car stops and two people get out. As they draw close to the Prophet, he says "Greetings in the name of the Lord."

"Greetings Prophet, and Benjamin you as well; in the name of the Lord shalom", the Rev answered as Mac comes up beside him.

Mac and the Rev stand alongside the Sage Brush prophet. They look at him and Mac says, "We finally know the truth, or should I say I do, the fight is on Prophet"

The Prophet smiles as he looks at both Mac and the Rev and then changes expressions saying soberly, "Tonight is a dark night for America and the world!"

Mac and the Rev looked a little puzzled and joined in with "but Project Black light and Alpha base was destroyed. Not to mention the Colonel is dead; that threat is gone!"

"Yes, you destroyed Alpha Base, but Project black light is alive and well. They meet right now beneath the Pentagon and worship their leader Lucifer. It is written that he should arise and it shall come to pass. The destruction of Alpha Base was part of their plan as was the Colonels Death. They will use all of this, including the fighting to bring in martial law and controls. Darkness isn't coming; it is here! America is theirs and they will take it over."

"What do we do then?" Asked Mac

"Nothing, everything in the Lords timing, prepare the Remnant for that which comes. It will come soon enough, but be sure it is not over! Before this comes to a permanent end in America, I am here to tell you that the Lord will make away for the Remnant to escape." The Prophet stopped and looked at them both, then continued "Just wait my friends, thank the Lord and seek him; and also go fishing", with that the Prophet smiled and said, "go in peace and his blessing!"

Mac heard something behind them and turned to see what it was. As he did the Rev looked also and saw some Antelope running behind them. The Rev and Mac watch them run free and enjoying the open space. Then they both turned around in time to see the Prophet was getting in his car.

"What, no disappearing tonight, no vanishing, you are actually leaving in a car?" Mac Smiled and saw the Prophet smile back "No, it is a beautiful night, a good night for a drive, huh Benjamin?"

"Benjamin looked at the Prophet and then to the others saying "Yes, it is a good night for a drive, are you ready Prophet?"

"Yes Benjamin, I am ready, good bye to you Rev and to you Mac, again walk in faith and be at peace my brothers, we will be in touch"

The Prophet turned to Benjamin and nodded saying "Okay, move on out when you're ready."

As they drove away, Mac and the Rev watched the Car disappear of sight. They looked around and listened as noises of the night sounded all around them. The night was clear and the stars shining, "Thank you Lord, for another night, and another day which comes" Mac stopped and smiled, then the Rev said, "And thank you Lord for your servants who have helped us, delivering us from our enemies." They both turned and got in the car and began the long journey back to the Ranch. It would be dawn before they get home, but they would enjoy the night and the presence of the Lord. They both were thankful, and believed that in the days to come, the deliverance of the Lord would be strong on their behalf against any enemy they faced."

The End of Steel the Darkness

Stay tuned for the next book in this series, The Steel Curtain: Around America, it is tight, there is no escape. The plan begins to unfold as both Operation Viper and Project Black Light holds America in its grip. The nation becomes surrounded by a Steel Curtain, with no escape and no way out. It is inevitable; many have lost hope as the plans of darkness are well laid out. They are moving forward efficiently. There is a problem though; powers who are opposed to what is happening. The lines form and the battle will soon begin in earnest. Who will win and when will it all be over. In the wings the Dark one waits and plots. The world is his and he knows it!

The End of Steel the Darkness

Stay tuned for more in this series!

Thank you for taking time to read this Journey, this story, and this work!

Mr. Dana G. Smith

For Booking or information on the prophetic end times visit:

www.DanaGlennSmith.com

www.Warn-Usa.com